THE
TWO VANREVELS

BOOTH TARKINGTON

1st WORLD
LIBRARY
Literary Society

The Two Vanrevels

Booth Tarkington

© 1st World Library, 2007
PO Box 2211
Fairfield, IA 52556
www.1stworldlibrary.com
First Edition

LCCN: 2007934105

Softcover ISBN: 978-1-4218-9620-5
Hardcover ISBN: 978-1-4218-9720-2
eBook ISBN: 978-1-4218-9520-8

Purchase *"The Two Vanrevels"*
as a traditional bound book at:
www.1stWorldLibrary.com/purchase.asp?ISBN=978-1-4218-9620-5

1st World Library is a literary, educational organization
dedicated to:

- Creating a free internet library of downloadable ebooks

- Hosting writing competitions and offering book publishing
scholarships.

1st World Library Literary Society

Giving Back to the World

"If you want to work on the core problem, it's early school literacy."

- James Barksdale, former CEO of Netscape

"No skill is more crucial to the future of a child, or to a democratic and prosperous society, than literacy."

- Los Angeles Times

"Literacy... means far more than learning how to read and write... The aim is to transmit... knowledge and promote social participation."

- UNESCO

"Literacy is not a luxury, it is a right and a responsibility. If our world is to meet the challenges of the twenty-first century we must harness the energy and creativity of all our citizens."

- President Bill Clinton

"Parents should be encouraged to read to their children, and teachers should be equipped with all available techniques for teaching literacy, so the varying needs and capacities of individual kids can be taken into account."

- Hugh Mackay

TABLE OF CONTENTS

CHAPTER I

A CAT CAN DO MORE THAN LOOK AT A KING

It was long ago in the days when men sighed when they fell in love; when people danced by candle and lamp, and did dance, too, instead of solemnly gliding about; in that mellow time so long ago, when the young were romantic and summer was roses and wine, old Carewe brought his lovely daughter home from the convent to wreck the hearts of the youth of Rouen.

That was not a far journey; only an afternoon's drive through the woods and by the river, in an April, long ago; Miss Betty's harp carefully strapped behind the great lumbering carriage, her guitar on the front seat, half-buried under a mound of bouquets and oddly shaped little bundles, farewell gifts of her comrades and the good Sisters. In her left hand she clutched a small lace handkerchief, with which she now and then touched her eyes, brimmed with the parting from Sister Cecilia, Sister Mary Bazilede, the old stone steps and all the girls: but for every time that she lifted the dainty kerchief to brush away the edge of a tear, she took a deep breath of the Western woodland air and smiled at least twice; for the years of strict inclosure within St. Mary's walls and still gardens were finished and done with, and at last the many-colored world flashed and danced in a mystery before her. This mystery was brilliant to the convent-girl because it contained men; she was eager to behold it.

They rumbled into town after sunset, in the fair twilight, the dogs barking before them, and everyone would have been surprised to know that Tom Vanrevel, instead of Mr. Crailey Gray, was the first to see her. By the merest accident, Tom was strolling near the Carewe place at the time; and when the carriage swung into the gates, with rattle and clink and clouds of dust at the finish, it was not too soon lost behind the shrubbery and trees for Tom to catch something more than a glimpse of a gray skirt behind a mound of flowers, and of a charming face with parted lips and dark eyes beneath the scuttle of an enormous bonnet. It happened— perhaps it is more accurate to say that Tom thought it happened - that she was just clearing away her veil when he turned to look. She blushed suddenly, so much was not to be mistaken; and the eyes that met his were remarkable for other reasons than the sheer loveliness of them, in that, even in the one flash of them he caught, they meant so many things at one time. They were sparkling, yet mournful; and they were wistful, although undeniably lively with the gayest comprehension of the recipient of their glance, seeming to say, "Oh, it's you, young man, is it!" And they were shy and mysterious with youth, full of that wonder at the world which has the appearance, sometimes, of wisdom gathered in the unknown out of which we came. But, above all, these eyes were fully conscious of Tom Vanrevel.

Without realizing what he did, Mr. Vanrevel stopped short. He had been swinging a walkingstick, which, describing a brief arc, remained poised half-way in its descent. There was only that one glance between them; and the carriage disappeared, leaving a scent of spring flowers in the air.

The young man was left standing on the wooden pavement

in the midst of a great loneliness, yet enveloped in the afterglow, his soul roseate, his being quavering, his expression, like his cane, instantaneously arrested. With such promptitude and finish was he disposed of, that, had Miss Carewe been aware of his name and the condition wrought in him by the single stroke, she could have sought only the terse Richard of England for a like executive ability, "Off with his head! So much for Vanrevel!"

She had lifted a slender hand to the fluttering veil, a hand in a white glove with a small lace gauntlet at the wrist. This gesture was the final divinity of the radiant vision which remained with the dazed young man as he went down the street; and it may have been three-quarters of an hour later when the background of the picture became vivid to him: a carefully dressed gentleman with heavy brows and a handsome high nose, who sat stiffly upright beside the girl, his very bright eyes quite as conscious of the stricken pedestrian as were hers, vastly different, however, in this: that they glittered, nay, almost bristled, with hostility; while every polished button of his blue coat seemed to reflect their malignancy, and to dart little echoing shafts of venom at Mr. Vanrevel.

Tom was dismayed by the acuteness of his perception that a man who does not speak to you has no right to have a daughter like the lady in the carriage; and, the moment of this realization occurring as he sat making a poor pretence to eat his evening meal at the "Rouen House," he dropped his fork rattling upon his plate and leaned back, staring at nothing, a proceeding of which his table-mate, Mr. William Cummings, the editor of the Rouen Journal, was too busy over his river bass to take note.

"Have you heard what's new in town?" asked Cummings presently, looking up.

"No," said Tom truthfully, for he had seen what was new, but not heard it.

"Old Carewe's brought his daughter home. Fanchon Bareaud was with her at St. Mary's until last year and Fanchon says she's not only a great beauty but a great dear."

"Ah!" rejoined the other with masterly indifference. "Dare say—dare say."

"No wonder you're not interested," said Cummings cheerfully, returning to the discussion of his bass. "The old villain will take precious good care you don't come near her."

Mr. Vanrevel already possessed a profound conviction to the same effect. Robert Meilhac Carewe was known not only as the wealthiest citizen of Rouen, but also as its heartiest and most steadfast hater: and, although there were only five or six thousand inhabitants, neither was a small distinction. For Rouen was ranked, in those easy days, as a wealthy town; even as it was called an old town; proud of its age and its riches, and bitter in its politics, of course. The French had built a fort there, soon after LaSalle's last voyage, and, as Crailey Gray said, had settled the place, and had then been settled themselves by the pioneer militia. After the Revolution, Carolinians and Virginians had come, by way of Tennessee and Kentucky; while the adventurous countrymen from Connecticut, travelling thither to sell, remained to buy— and then sell—when the country was in its teens. In course of time the little trading-post of the Northwest Territory had grown to be the leading centre of elegance and culture in the Ohio Valley—at least they said so in Rouen; only a few people in the country, such as Mr. Irving of Tarrytown, for instance, questioning whether a centre could lead.

The pivotal figure, though perhaps not the heart, of this centre, was unquestionably Mr. Carewe, and about him the neat and tight aristocracy of the place revolved; the old French remnant, having liberally intermarried, forming the nucleus, together with descendants of the Cavaliers (and those who said they were) and the industrious Yankees, by virtue (if not by the virtues) of all whom, the town grew and prospered. Robert Carewe was Rouen's magnate, commercially and socially, and, until an upstart young lawyer named Vanrevel struck into his power with a broad-axe, politically. The wharves were Carewe's; the warehouses that stood by the river, and the line of packets which plied upon it, were his; half the town was his, and in Rouen this meant that he was possessed of the Middle Justice, the High and the Low. His mother was a Frenchwoman, and, in those days, when to go abroad was a ponderous and venturesome undertaking, the fact that he had spent most of his youth in the French capital wrought a certain glamour about him; for to the American, Paris was Europe, and it lay shimmering on the far horizon of every imagination, a golden city. Scarce a drawing-room in Rouen lacked its fearsome engraving entitled "Grand Ball at the Tuileries," nor was Godey's Magazine ever more popular than when it contained articles elaborate of similar scenes of festal light, where brilliant uniforms mingled with shining jewels, fair locks, and the white shoulders of magnificently dressed duchesses, countesses, and ladies. Credit for this description should be given entirely to the above-mentioned periodical. Furthermore, a sojourn in Paris was held to confer a "certain nameless and indescribable polish" upon the manners of the visitor; also, there was something called "an air of foreign travel."

They talked a great deal about polish in those days; and some examples still extant do not deny their justification; but in the case of Mr. Carewe, there existed a citizen of Rouen, one already quoted, who had the temerity to declare the polish to be in truth quite nameless and indescribable for the reason that one cannot paint a vacuum. However, subscription to this opinion should not be over-hasty, since Mr. Crailey Gray had been notoriously a rival of Carewe's with every pretty woman in town, both having the same eye in such matters, and also because the slandered gentleman could assume a manner when he chose to, whether or not he possessed it. At his own table he exhaled a hospitable graciousness which, from a man of known evil temper, carried the winsomeness of surprise. When he wooed, it was with an air of stately devotion, combined with that knowingness which sometimes offsets for a widower the tendency a girl has to giggle at him; and the combination had been, once or twice, too much for even the alluring Crailey.

Mr. Carewe lived in an old-fashioned house on the broad, quiet, shady street which bore his name. There was a wide lawn in front, shadowy under elm and locust trees, and bounded by thick shrubberies. A long garden, fair with roses and hollyhocks, lay outside the library windows, an old-time garden, with fine gravel paths and green arbors; drowsed over in summer-time by the bees, while overhead the locust rasped his rusty cadences the livelong day; and a faraway sounding love-note from the high branches brought to mind the line, like an old refrain:

"The voice of the turtle was heard in the land."

Between the garden and the carriage gates there was a fountain where a bronze boy with the dropsy (but not minding it) lived in a perpetual bath from a green goblet held over his head. Nearby, a stone sun-dial gleamed against a clump of lilac bushes; and it was upon this spot that the white kitten introduced Thomas Vanrevel to Miss Carewe.

Upon the morning after her arrival, having finished her

piano-forte practice, touched her harp twice, and arpeggioed the Spanish Fandango on her guitar, Miss Betty read two paragraphs of "Gilbert" (for she was profoundly determined to pursue her tasks with diligence), but the open windows disclosing a world all sunshine and green leaves, she threw the book aside with a good conscience, and danced out to the garden. There, coming upon a fuzzy, white ball rolling into itself spirally on a lazy pathway, she pounced at it, whereupon the thing uncurled with lightning swiftness, and fled, more like a streak than a kitten, down the drive, through the open gates and into the street, Miss Betty in full cry.

Across the way there chanced to be strolling a young lady in blue, accompanied by a gentleman whose leisurely gait gave no indication of the maneuvering he had done to hasten their walk into its present direction. He was apparently thirty or thirty-one, tall, very straight, dark, smooth-shaven, his eyes keen, deep-set, and thoughtful, and his high white hat, white satin cravat, and careful collar, were evidence of an elaboration of toilet somewhat unusual in Rouen for the morning; also, he was carrying a pair of white gloves in his hand and dangled a slender ebony cane from his wrist. The flying kitten headed toward the couple, when, with a celerity only to be accounted for on the theory that his eye had been fixed on the Carewe gateway for some time previous to this sudden apparition, the gentleman leaped in front of the fugitive.

The kitten attempted a dodge to pass; the gentleman was there before it. The kitten feinted; the gentleman was altogether too much on the spot. Immediately—and just as Miss Carewe, flushed and glowing, ran into the street—the small animal doubled, evaded Miss Betty's frantic clutch, re-entered the gateway, and attempted a disappearance into the lilac bushes, instead of going round them, only to find itself, for a fatal two seconds, in difficulties with the close-set thicket of stems.

In regard to the extraordinary agility of which the pursuing gentleman as capable, it is enough to say that he caught the cat. He emerged from the lilacs holding it in one hand, his gloves and white hat in the other, and presented himself before Miss Betty with a breathlessness not entirely attributable to his exertions.

For a moment, as she came running toward him and he met her flashing look, bright with laughter and recognition and haste, he stammered. A thrill nothing less than delirious sent the blood up behind his brown cheeks, for he saw that she, too, knew that this was the second time their eyes had met. Naturally, at that time he could not know how many other gentlemen were to feel that same thrill (in their cases, also, delirious, no less) with the same, accompanying, mysterious feeling, which came just before Miss Betty's lashes fell, that one had found, at last, a precious thing, lost long since in childhood, or left, perhaps, upon some other planet in a life ten thousand years ago.

He could not speak at once, but when he could, "Permit me, madam," he said solemnly, offering the captive, "to restore your kitten."

An agitated kitten should not be detained by clasping its waist, and already the conqueror was paying for his victory. There ensued a final, outrageous squirm of despair; two frantic claws, extended, drew one long red mark across the stranger's wrist and another down the back of his hand to the knuckles. They were good, hearty scratches, and the blood followed the artist's lines rapidly; but of this the young man took no note, for he knew that be was about to hear Miss Carewe's voice for the first time.

"They say the best way to hold them," he observed, "is by the scruff of the neck."

Beholding his wounds, suffered in her cause, she gave a pitying cry that made his heart leap with the richness and sweetness of it. Catching the kitten from him, she dropped it to the ground in such wise as to prove nature's foresight most kind in cushioning the feet of cats.

"Ah! I didn't want it that much!"

"A cat in the hand is worth two nightingales in the bush," he said boldly, and laughed. "I would shed more blood than that!"

Miss Betty blushed like a southern dawn, and started back from him. From the convent but yesterday—and she had taken a man's hand in both of hers!

It was to this tableau that the lady in blue entered, following the hunt through the gates, where she stopped with a discomposed countenance. At once, however, she advanced, and with a cry of greeting, enveloped Miss Betty in a brief embrace, to the relief of the latter's confusion. It was Fanchon Bareaud, now two years emancipated from St. Mary's, and far gone in taffeta. With her lustreful light hair, absent blue eyes, and her gentle voice, as small and pretty as her face and figure, it was not too difficult to justify Crailey Gray's characterization of her as one of those winsome baggages who had made an air of feminine helplessness the fashion of the day.

It is a wicked thing that some women should kiss when a man is by; in the present instance the gentleman became somewhat faint.

"I'm so glad—glad!" exclaimed Betty. "You were just coming to see me, weren't you? My father is in the library. Let me—"

Miss Bareaud drew back. "No, no!" she interrupted hastily and with evident perturbation. "I—we must be on our way immediately." She threw a glance at the gentleman, which let him know that she now comprehended his gloves, and why their stroll had trended toward Carewe Street. "Come at once!" she commanded him quickly, in an undertone.

"But now that you're here," said Miss Betty, wondering very much why he was not presented to her, "won't you wait and let me gather a nosegay for you? Our pansies and violets—"

"I could help," the gentleman suggested, with the look of a lame dog at Miss Bareaud. "I have been considered useful about a garden."

"Fool!" Betty did not hear the word that came from Miss Bareaud's closed teeth, though she was mightily surprised at the visible agitation of her schoolmate, for the latter's face was pale and excited. And Miss Carewe's amazement was complete when Fanchon, without more words, cavalierly seized the gentleman's arm and moved toward the street with him as rapidly as his perceptible reluctance to leave permitted. But at the gate Miss Bareaud turned and called back over her shoulder, as if remembering the necessity of offering an excuse for so remarkable a proceeding: "I shall come again very soon. Just now we are upon an errand of great importance. Good-day!"

Miss Betty waved her hand, staring after them, her eyes large with wonder. She compressed her lips tightly: "Errand!" This was the friend of childhood's happy hour, and they had not met in two years!

"Errand!" She ran to the hedge, along the top of which a high white hat was now seen perambulating; she pressed down a loose branch, and called in a tender voice to the stranger whom Fanchon had chosen should remain nameless:

"Be sure to put some salve on your hand!"

He made a bow which just missed being too low, but did miss it.

"It is there—already," he said; and, losing his courage after the bow, made his speech with so palpable a gasp before the last word that the dullest person in the world could have seen that he meant it.

Miss Betty disappeared.

There was a rigidity of expression about the gentle mouth of Fanchon Bareaud, which her companion did not enjoy, as they went on their way, each preserving an uneasy silence, until at her own door, she turned sharply upon him. "Tom Vanrevel, I thought you were the steadiest—and now you've proved yourself the craziest—soul in Rouen!" she burst out. "And I couldn't say worse!"

"Why didn't you present me to her?" asked Vanrevel.

"Because I thought a man of your gallantry might prefer not to face a shotgun in the presence of ladies!"

"Pooh!"

"Pooh!" mimicked Miss Bareaud. "You can 'pooh' as much as you like, but if he had seen us from the window—" She covered her face with her hands for a moment, then dropped them and smiled upon him. "I understand perfectly to what I owe the pleasure of a stroll with you this morning, and your casual insistence on the shadiness of Carewe Street!" He laughed nervously, but her smile vanished, and she continued, "Keep away, Tom. She is beautiful, and at St. Mary's I always thought she had spirit and wit, too. I only hope Crailey won't see her before the wedding! But it isn't safe for you. Go along, now, and ask Crailey please to come at three this afternoon."

This message from Mr. Gray's betrothed was not all the ill-starred Tom conveyed to his friend. Mr. Vanrevel was ordinarily esteemed a person of great reserve and discretion; nevertheless there was one man to whom he told everything, and from whom he had no secrets. He spent the noon hour in feeble attempts to describe to Crailey Gray the outward appearance of Miss Elizabeth Carewe; how she ran like a young Diana; what one felt upon hearing her voice; and he presented in himself an example exhibiting something of the cost of looking in her eyes. His conversation was more or less incoherent, but the effect of it was complete.

CHAPTER II

SURVIVING EVILS OF THE REIGN OF TERROR

Does there exist an incredulous, or jealous, denizen of another portion of our country who, knowing that the room in the wooden cupola over Mr. Carewe's library was commonly alluded to by Rouen as the "Tower Chamber," will prove himself so sectionally prejudiced as to deny that the town was a veritable hotbed of literary interest, or that Sir 'Walter Scott was ill-appreciated there? Some of the men looked sly, and others grinned, at mention of this apartment; but the romantic were not lacking who spoke of it in whispers: how the lights sometimes shone there all night long, and the gentlemen drove away, whitefaced, in the dawn. The cupola, rising above the library, overlooked the garden; and the house, save for that, was of a single story, with a low veranda running the length of its front. The windows of the library and of a row of bedrooms—one of which was Miss Betty's—lined the veranda, "steamboat fashion;" the inner doors of these rooms all opening upon a long hail which bisected the house. he stairway leading to the room in the cupola rose the library itself, while the bisecting hail afforded be only access to the library; hence, the gossips, 'eli acquainted with the geography of the place, conferred seriously together upon what effect Miss Betty's homecoming would have in this connection:

Dr anyone going to the stairway must needs pass her door; and, what was more to the point, a party C gentlemen descending late from the mysterious garret might be not so quiet as they intended, and the young lady sufficiently disturbed to inquire of her father what entertainment he provided that should keep his guests until four in the morning.

But at present it was with the opposite end of the house that the town was occupied, for there, workmen were hammering and sawing and painting day long, finishing the addition Mr. Carewe was building for his daughter's debut. This hammering disturbed Miss Betty, who had become almost as busy with the French Revolution as with her mantua-maker. For she had found in her father's library many books not for convent-shelves; and she had become a Girondin. She found memoirs, histories, and tales of that delectable period, then not so dim with time but that the figures of it were more than tragic shadows; and for a week there was no meal in that house to which she sat down earlier than half an hour Jate. She had a rightful property-interest in the Revolution, her own great-uncle having been one of those who "suffered;" not, however, under the guillotine; for to Georges Meilhac appertained the rare distinction of death by accident on the day when the business-like young Bonaparte played upon the mob with his cannon.

There were some yellow letters of this great uncle's in a box which had belonged to her grandmother, a rich discovery for Miss Betty, who read and re-read them with eager and excited eyes, living more in Paris with Georges and his friends than in Rouen with her father. Indeed, she had little else to do. Mr. Carewe was no comrade for her, by far the reverse. She seldom saw him, except at the table, when he sat with averted eyes, and talked to her very little; and, while making elaborate preparation for her introduction to his friends (such was his phrase) he treated her with a perfunctory civility which made her wonder if her advent was altogether welcome to him; bat when she noticed that his hair looked darker than usual about every fourth day, she began to understand Why he appeared ungrateful to her for growing up. He went out a great deal, though no visitors came to the house; for it was known that Mr. Carewe desired to present his daughter to no one until he presented her to all. Fanchon Bareaud, indeed, made one hurried and embarrassed call, evading Miss Betty's reference to the chevalier of the kitten with a dexterity too nimble to be thought unintentional. Miss Carewe was forbidden to return her friend's visit until after her debut; and Mr. Carewe explained that there was always some worthless Young men hanging about the Bareaud's, where (he did not add) they interfered with a worthy oh one who desired to honor Fanchon's older sister, Virginia, with his attentions.

This was no great hardship for Miss Betty, as, since plunging into the Revolution with her great-uncle, she had lost some curiosity concerning the men of to-day, doubting that they would show forth as heroic, as debonnair, gay and tragic as he. He was the legendary hero of her childhood; she remembered her mother's stories of him perhaps more clearly than she remembered her mother; and one of the older Sisters had known him in Paris and had talked of him at length, giving the flavor of his dandyism and his beauty at first hand to his young relative. He had been one of those hardy young men wearing unbelievable garments, who began to appear in the garden of the Tuileries with knives in their sleeves and cudgels in their hands, about April, 1794, and whose dash and recklessness in many matters were the first intimations that the Citizen Tallien was about to cause the Citizen Robespierre to shoot himself through the jaw.

In the library hung a small, full-length drawing of Georges, done in color by Miss Betty's grandmother; and this she carried to her own room an& studied long and ardently, until sometimes the man himself seemed to stand before her, in spite of the fact that Mile. Meithac had not a distinguished talent and M. Meilhac's features might have been anybody's. It was to be seen, however, that he was smiling.

Miss Betty had an impression that her grandmother's art of portraiture would have been more-successful with the profile than the "full-face." Nevertheless, nothing could be more clearly indicated than that the hair of M. Melihac was very yellow, and his short, huge-lapeiled waistcoat white, striped with scarlet. An enormous cravat coyered his chin; the heavy collar of his yellow coat rose behind his ears, while its tails fell to his ankles; and the tight trousers of white and yellow stripes were tied with white ribbons about the middle of the calf; he wore white stockings and gold-buckled yellow shoes, and on the back of his head a jauntily cocked black hat. Miss Betty innocently wondered why his letters did not speak of P,tion, of Vergniaud, or of Dumoriez, since in the historical novels which she read, the hero's lot was inevitably linked with that of everyone of importance in his generation; yet Georges appeared to have been unacquainted with these personages, Robespierre being the only name of cones-quence mentioned in his letters; and then it appeared in much the same fashion practised by her father in alluding to the Governor of the State, who had the misfortune to be unpopular with Mr. Carewe. But this did not dim her great-uncle's lustre in Miss Betty's eyes, nor lessen for her the pathetic romance of the smile he wore.

Beholding this smile, one remembered the end to which his light footsteps bad led him; and it was unavoidable to picture him left lying in the empty street behind the heels of the flying crowd, carefully forming that same smile on his lips, and taking much pride in passing with some small, cynical speech, murmured to himself, concerning the mutility of a gentleman's getting shot by his friends for merely being present to applaud them. So, fancying him thus, with his yellow hair, his scarletitriped waistcoat, and his tragedy, the young girl felt a share of family greatness, or, at least, of picturesqueness, descend to her. And she smiled sadly back upon the smile in the picture, and dreamed about its original night after night.

Whether or no another figure, that of a dark young man in a white hat, with a white kitten etching his wrist in red, found any place in her dreams. at this period, - it is impossible to determine. She did not see him again. it is quite another thing, hazardous to venture, to state that he did not see her. At all events, it is certain that many people who bad never beheld her were talking of her; that Rouen was full of contention concerning her beauty and her gift of music, for a song can be heard through an open window. And how did it happen that Crailey Gray knew that it was Miss Carewe's habit to stroll in her garden for half an hour or so, each evening before retiring, and that she went to mass every morning soon after sunrise? Crailey Gray never rose at, or near, sunrise in his life, though he sometimes beheld it, from another point of view, as the end of the evening. It appears that someone must have told him.

One night when the moon lay white on the trees and housetops, Miss Betty paused in her evening promenade and seated herself upon a bench on the borders of the garden, "touched," as the books of the time would have put it, "by the sweet tranquillity of the scene," and wrought upon by the tender incentive to sighs and melancholy which youth in loneliness finds in a loveliness of the earth. The breeze bore the smells of the old-fashioned garden, of violets and cherry blossoms, and a sound of distant violins came on the air playing the new song from the new opera.

"But I also dreamt, which pleased me most, That you loved me just the same—"

they sang; and with the lilt of them and the keen beauty of the night, the inherited pain of the ages rose from the depths of the young girl's heart, so that she thought it must break; for what reason she could not have told, since she was without care or sorrow that she knew, except the French Revolution, yet tears shone upon the long lashes. She shook them off and looked up with a sudden odd consciousness. The next second she sprang to her feet with a gasp and a choked outcry, her bands pressed to her breast.

Ten paces in front of her, a gap in the shrubbery where tall trees rose left a small radiant area of illumination like that of a lime-light in a theatre, its brilliancy intensified by the dark foliage behind. It was open to view only from the bench by which she stood, and appeared, indeed, like the stage of a little theatre a stage occupied by a bizarre figure. For, in the centre of this shining patch, with the light strong on his face, was standing a fair-haired young man, dressed in a yellow coat, a scarlet and white striped waistcoat, wearing a jauntily cocked black hat on his bead. And even to the last detail, the ribbon laces above the ankle and the gold-buckled shoes, be was the sketch of Georges Meilhac sprung into life.

About this slender figure there hung a wan sweetness like a fine mist, almost an ethereality in that light; yet in the pale face lurked something reckless, something of the actor, too; and though his smile was gentle and wistful, there was a twinkle behind it, not seen at first, something amused and impish; a small surprise underneath, like a flea in a rose-jar.

Fixed to the spot by this apparition, Miss Betty stood wildly staring, her straining eyelids showing the white above and below the large brown iris. Her breath came faster and deeper, until, between her parted lips it became vocal in a quick sound like a sob. At that he spoke.

"Forgive me!" The voice was low, vibrant,

and so exceedingly musical that he might have been accused of coolly selecting his best tone; and it became only sweeter when, even more softly, in a semi-whisper of almost crucial pleading, he said, "Ah—don't go away!"

In truth, she could not go; she had been too vitally stirred; she began to tremble excessively, and sank back upon the bench, motioning him away with vague gestures of her shaking hands.

This was more than the Incroyable had counted upon, and far from his desires. He started forward with an exclamation.

"Don't come near me!" she gasped. "Who are you? Go away!"

"Give me one second to explain," he began; but with the instant reassurance of this beginning she cut him off short, her fears dispelled by his commonplace. Nay, indignation displaced them so quickly that she fairly flashed up before him to her full height.

"You did not come in by the gate!" she cried. "What do you mean by coming here in that dress What right have you in my garden?"

"Just one word," he begged quickly, but very gently. "You'd allow a street-beggar that much!"

She stood before him, panting, and, as he thought, glorious, in her flush of youth and anger. Tom Vanrevel had painted her incoherently, but richly, in spite of that, his whole heart being in the portrait; and - Crailey Gray had smiled at what he deemed the exaggeration of an ordinarily unimpressionable man who had fallen in love "at first sight;" yet, in the presence of the reality, the Incroyable decided that Tom's colors had been gray and humble. It was not that she was merely lovely, that her nose was straight, and her chin dexterously wrought between square and oval; that her dark hair lay soft as a shadow on her white brow; not that the trembling hand she held against her breast sprang from a taper wrist and tapered again to the tips of the long fingers; nor that she was of that slenderness as strong as it is delicate; not all the exquisite regularity of line and mould, nor simplicity of color, gave her that significance which made the Incroyable declare to himself that he stood for the first time in the presence of Beauty, and that now he knew the women he had been wont to call beautiful were but pretty. And yet her beauty, he told himself, was the least of her loveliness, for there was a glamour about her. It was not only the richness of her youth; but there was an ineffable exhalation which seemed to be made partly of light, partly of the very spirit of her, and, oddly enough, partly of the scent of the little fan that hung by a ribbon from her waist. This was a woman like a wine, he felt, there was a bouquet.

In regard to the bouquet of the young man himself, if he possessed one, it is pertinent to relate that at this very instant the thought skipped across his mind (like the hop of a flea in a rose-jar) that some day he might find the moment when he could tell her the truth about herself—with a half-laugh— and say: "The angels sent their haloes in a sandal-wood box to be made into a woman—and it was you!"

"If - you have anything to say for yourself, say it quickly!" said Miss Betty.

"You were singing a while ago," he answered, somewhat huskily, "and I stopped on the street to listen; then I came here to be nearer. The spell of your voice " He broke off abruptly to change the word. "The spell of the song came over me—it is my dearest favorite—so that I stood afterward in a sort of trance, only hearing again, in the silence, 'The stolen heart, like the gathered rose, will bloom but for a day!' I did not see you until you came to the bench. You must believe me: I would not have frightened you for anything in the world."

"Why are you wearing that dress?"

He laughed, and pointed to where, behind him on the ground, lay a long gray cloak, upon which had been tossed a white mask. "I'm on my way to the masquerade;" he answered, with an airy gesture in the direction of the violins. "I'm an Incroyable, you see; and I had the costume made from my recollection of a sketch of your great-uncle. I saw it a long time ago in your library."

Miss Carewe's accustomed poise was quite recovered; indeed, she was astonished to discover a distinct trace of disappointment that the brilliant apparition must offer so tame an explanation. What he said was palpably the truth; there was a masquerade that night, she knew, at the Madrillon's, a little way up Carewe Street, and her father had gone, an hour earlier, a blue domino over his arm.

The Incroyable was a person of almost magical perceptiveness; he felt the let-down immediately and feared a failure. This would not do; the attitude of tension between them must be renewed at once. "You'll forgive me?" he began, in a quickly impassioned tone. "It was only after you sang, a dream possessed me, and—"

"I cannot stay to talk with you," Miss Betty interrupted, and added, with a straightforwardness which made him afraid she would prove lamentably direct: "I do not know you."

Perhaps she remembered that already one young man had been presented to her by no better sponsor than a white cat, and had no desire to carry her unconventionality farther than that. In the present instance there was not even a kitten.

She turned toward the house, whereupon he gave a little pathetic exclamation - of pleading in a voice that was masterly, being as sincere as it was musical, and he took a few leaning steps toward her, both hands outstretched.

"One moment more!" he cried, as she turned again to him. "It may be the one chance of my life to speak with you; don't deny me this. - All the rest will meet you when the happy evening comes, will dance with you, talk with you, see you when they like, listen to you sing. I, alone, must hover about the gates, or steal like a thief into your garden to hear you from a distance. Listen to me—just this once—for a moment?"

"I cannot listen," she said firmly; and stood quite still. She was now in deep shadow.

"I will not believe you merciless! You would not condemn the meanest criminal unheard I" Remembering that she was so lately from the convent, he ventured this speech in a deep, thrilling voice, only to receive a distinct shock for his pains, for she greeted it with an irrepressible, most unexpected peal of contralto laughter, and his lips parted slightly with the surprise of it.

They parted much farther in the next instant—in good truth, it may be stated of the gentleman that he was left with his mouth open—for, suddenly leaning toward him out of the shadow into the light, her face shining as a cast of tragedy, she cried in a hoarse whisper:

"Are you a murderer?"

And with that and a whisk of her skirts, and a footfall on the gravel path, she was gone. He stood dumbfounded, poor comedian, having come to play the chief role, but to find the scene taken out of his hands. Then catching the flutter of her wrap, as she disappeared into the darkness of the veranda, be cried in a loud, manly voice:

"You are a dear!"

As he came out into the street through a gap in the hedge, he paused, drawing his cloak about him, and lifted his face to the eastern moon. It was a strange face: the modelling most like what is called "Greek," save for the nose, which was a trifle too short for that, and the features showed a happy purity of outline almost childlike; the blue eyes, clear, fleckless, serenely irresponsible, with more the look of refusing responsibility than being unconscious of it; eyes without care, without prudence, and without evil. A stranger might have said be was about twenty-five and had never a thought in his life. There were some blossoms on the hedge, and he touched one lightly, as though he chucked it under the chin; he smiled upon it then, but not as he had smiled upon Miss Betty, for this was his own, the smile that came when he was alone; and, when it came, the face was no longer joyous as it had been in repose; there was an infinite patience and worn tolerance-possibly for himself. This incongruous and melancholy smile was astonishing: one looked for the laughter of a boy and found, instead, a gentle, worldly, old prelate.

Standing there, all alone in the moonlight, by the hedge, he lifted both hands high and waved them toward the house, as children wave to each other across lawns at twilight. After that he made a fantastic bow to his corrugated shadow on the board sidewalk.

"Again, you rogue!" be exclaimed aloud. Then, as he faced about and began to walk in the direction of the beckoning violins: "I wonder if Tom's kitten was better, after all!"

CHAPTER III

THE ROGUE'S GALLERY OF A FATHER SHOULD BE EXHIBITED TO A DAUGHTER WITH PARTICULAR CARE

Those angels appointed to be guardians of the merry people of Rouen, poising one night, between earth and stars, discovered a single brilliant and resonant spot, set in the midst of the dark, quiet town like a jewelled music-box on a black cloth. Sounds of revelry and the dance from the luminous spot came up through the summer stillness to the weary guardians all night long, until, at last, when a red glow stole into the east, and the dance still continued, nay, grew faster than ever, the celestial watchers found the work too heavy for their strength, and forthwith departed, leaving the dancers to their own devices; for, as everyone knows, when a dance lasts till daylight, guardian angels flee.

All night long the fiddles had been swinging away at their best; all night long the candles had shone in thin rows of bright orange through the slits of the window-blinds; but now, as the day broke over the maples, the shutters were flung open by laughing young men, and the drivers of the carriages, waiting in the dusty street, pressed up closer to the hedge, or came within and stretched themselves upon the lawn, to see the people waltzing in the daylight. The horses, having no such desires, stood with loosened check-reins, slightly twitching their upper lips, wistful of the tall grass which bordered the wooden sidewalk, though now and then one would lift his head high, sniffing the morning air and bending an earnest gaze not upon the dancers but upon the florid east.

Over the unwearied plaint of French-horn, violin, and bassoon, rose a silvery confusion of voices and laughter and the sound of a hundred footfalls in unison, while, from the open windows there issued a warm breath, heavily laden with the smell of scented fans, of rich fabrics, of dying roses, to mingle with the spicy perfume of a wild crab-tree in fullest blossom, which stood near enough to peer into the ball-room, and, like a brocaded belle herself, challenge the richest to show raiment as fine, the loveliest to look as fair and joyful in the dawn..

"Believe me, of all those endearing young charms, Which I gaze on so fondly to-day, Were to fade by to-morrow and fleet from my arms, Like fairy gifts fading away—"

So ran the violins in waltz time, so bassoon and horn to those dulcet measures; and then, with one accord, a hundred voices joined them in the old, sweet melody:

"Thou wouldst still be adored as this moment thou art, Let thy loveliness fade as it will; And around the dear ruin each wish of my heart Would entwine itself verdantly still."

And the jealous crab-tree found but one to overmatch itself in beauty: a lady who was the focus of the singing; for, by the time the shutters were flung open, there was not a young man in the room, lacked he never so greatly in music or in voice, who did not heartily desire to sing to Miss Betty Carewe, and who did not now (craning neck over partner's shoulder) seek to fix her with his glittering eye, while he sang "Oh, believe me" most directly and conspicuously at her. For that night was the beginning of Miss Betty's famous career as the belle of Rouen, and was the date from which strangers were to hear of her as "the beautiful Miss Carewe," until "beautiful" was left off, visitors to the town being supposed to have heard at least that much before they came.

There had been much discussion of her, though only one or two had caught glimpses of her; but most of the gallants appeared to agree with Crailey Gray, who aired his opinion—in an exceedingly casual way—at the little club on Main Street. Mr. Gray held that when the daughter of a man as rich as Bob Carewe was heralded as a beauty the chances were that she would prove disappointing, and, for his part, he was not even interested enough to attend and investigate. So he was going down the river in a canoe and preferred the shyness of bass to that of a girl of eighteen just from the convent, he said. Tom Vanrevel was not present on the occasion of these remarks; and the general concurrence with Crailey may be suspected as a purely verbal one, since, when the evening came, two of the most enthusiastic dancers and love-makers of the town, the handsome Tappingham Marsh and that doughty ex-dragoon and Indian fighter, stout old General Trumble, were upon the field before the enemy appeared; that is to say, they were in the new ball-room before their host; indeed, the musicians had not arrived, and Nelson, an aged negro servitor, was engaged in lighting the house.

The crafty pair had planned this early descent with a view to monopoly by right of priority, in case the game proved worth the candle, and they were leaning effectively against the little railing about the musicians' platform when Mr. Carewe entered the room with his daughter on his arm.

She was in white, touched with countless small lavender

flowers; there were rows and rows of wonderful silk and lace flounces on her skirt, and her fan hung from a rope of great pearls. Ah, hideous, blue, rough cloth of the convent, unforgotten, but laid aside forever, what a chrysalis you were!

Tappingham twitched his companion's sleeve, but the General was already posing; and neither heard the words of presentation, because Miss Betty gave each of them a quick look, then smiled upon them as they bowed; the slayers were prostrated before their prey. Never were lady-killers more instantaneously tamed and subjugated by the power of the feminine eye. Will Cummings came in soon, and, almost upon his heels, Eugene Madrillon and young Frank Chenoweth. No others appeared for half an hour, and the five gentlemen looked at one another aside, each divining his own diplomacy in his fellow's eye, and each laboriously explaining to the others his own mistake in regard to the hour designated upon Mr. Carewe's cards of invitation. This small embarrassment, however, did not prevent General Trumble and young Mr. Chenoweth from coming to high words over Miss Carewe's little, gilt-filigree "programme" of dances.

It may be not untimely to remark, also, of these five redoubtable beaux, that, during the evening, it occurred to every one of them to be glad that Crailey Gray was betrothed to Fanchon Bareaud, and that he was down on the Rouen River with a canoe, a rod and a tent. Nay, without more words, to declare the truth in regard to Crailey, they felt greater security in his absence from the field than in his betrothal. As Mr. Chenoweth, a youth as open as out-of-doors, both in countenance and mind, observed plaintively to Tappingham Marsh in a corner, while they watched Miss Betty's lavender flowers miraculously swirling through a quadrille: "Crailey, you know, well, Crailey's been engaged before!" It was not Mr. Chenoweth's habit to disguise his apprehensions, and Crailey Gray would not fish for bass forever.

The same Chenoweth was he, who, maddened by the General's triumphantly familiar way of toying with Miss Betty's fan between two dances, attempted to propose to her during the sunrise waltz. Having sung "Oh, believe me" in her ear as loudly as he could, he expressed the wish—quite as loudly—"That this waltz might last for always!"

That was the seventh time it had been said to Betty during the night, and though Mr. Chenoweth's predecessors had revealed their desires in a guise lacking this prodigious artlessness, she already possessed no novel acquaintance with the exclamation. But she made no comment; her partner's style was not a stimulant to repartee. "It would be heaven," he amplified earnestly, "it would be heaven to dance with you forever—on a desert isle where the others couldn't come!" he finished with sudden acerbity as his eye caught the General's.

He proceeded, and only the cessation of the music aided Miss Carewe in stopping the declaration before it was altogether out; and at that point Frank's own father came to her rescue, though in a fashion little saving of her confusion. The elder Chenoweth was one of the gallant and kindly Southern colony that made it natural for Rouen always to speak of Miss Carewe as "Miss Betty. He was a handsome old fellow, whose hair, long moustache and imperial were as white as he was proud of them, a Virginian with the admirable Southern fearlessness of being thought senti-mental. Mounting a chair with complete dignity, he lifted a glass of wine high in the air, and, when all the other glasses had been filled, proposed the health of his young hostess. He made a speech of some length, pronouncing himself quite as hopelessly in love with his old friend's daughter as all could see his own son was; and wishing her long life and prosperity, with many allusions to fragrant bowers and the Muses.

It made Miss Betty happy, but it was rather trying, too, for she could only stand with downcast eyes before them all, trembling a little, and receiving a mixed impression of Mr. Chenoweth's remarks, catching fragments here and there: "And may the blush upon that gentle cheek, lovelier than the radiant clouds at set of sun," and "Yet the sands of the hourglass must fall, and in the calm and beauteous old age some day to be her lot, when fond mem'ry leads her back to view again the brilliant scene about her now, where stand 'fair women and brave men,' winecup in hand to do her honor, oh, may she wipe the silent tear", and the like. As the old gentleman finished, and before the toast was drunk, Fanchon Bareaud, kissing her hand to Betty, took up the song again; and they all joined in, lifting their glasses to the blushing and happy girl clinging to her father's arm:

"Thou wouldst still be adored as this moment thou art, Let thy loveliness fade as it will; And around the dear ruin, each wish of my heart, Would entwine itself verdantly still."

They were happy people who had not learned to be self-conscious enough to fear doing a pretty thing openly without mocking themselves for it; and it was a brave circle they made about Betty Carewe, the charming faces of the women and their fine furbelows, handsome men and tall, all so gay, so cheerily smiling, and yet so earnest in their welcome to her. No one was afraid to "let out" his voice; their song went full and strong over the waking town, and when it was finished the ball was over, too.

The veranda and the path to the gate became like tropic gardens, the fair colors of the women's dresses, ballooning in the early breeze, making the place seem strewn with giant blossoms. They all went away at the same time, those in carriages calling farewells to each other and to the little processions departing on foot in different directions to homes near by. The sound of the voices and laughter drew away, slowly died out altogether, and the silence of the street was strange and unfamiliar to Betty. She went to the hedge and watched the musicians, who were the last to go, until they passed from sight: little black toilsome figures, carrying grotesque black boxes. While she could still see them, it seemed to her that her ball was not quite over, and she wished to hold the least speck of it as long as she could; but when they had disappeared, she faced the truth with a deep sigh: the long, glorious night was finished indeed.

What she needed now was another girl: the two would have gone to Betty's room and danced it all over again until noon; but she had only her father. She found him smoking a Principe cigar upon the veranda, so she seated herself timidly, nevertheless with a hopeful glance at him, on the steps at his feet; and, as she did so, he looked down upon her with something more akin to geniality than anything she had ever seen in his eye before. It was not geniality itself, but might be third cousin to it. Indeed, in his way, he was almost proud of her, though he had no wish to show it. Since one was compelled to display the fact that one possessed a grown daughter, it was well that she be like this one.

They did not know each other very well, and she often doubted that they would ever become intimate. There was no sense of companionship for either in the other; she had been unable to break through his perfunctory, almost formal, manner with her; therefore, because he encouraged no affection in her, she felt none, and wondered why, since he was her father. She was more curious about him than interested, and, though she did not know it, she was prepared to judge him—should occasion arise—precisely as she would judge any other mere acquaintance. This morning, for the first time, she was conscious of a sense of warmth and gratitude toward him: the elaborate fashion in which he had introduced her to his friends made it appear possible that he liked her; for he had forgotten nothing, and to remember everything in this case was to be lavish, which has often the appearance of generosity.

And yet there had been a lack: some small thing she had missed, though she was not entirely sure that she identified it; but the lack had not been in her father or in anything he had done. Then, too, there was something so unexpectedly human and pleasant in his not going to bed at once, but remaining to smoke on the veranda at this hour, that she gave him credit for a little of her own excitement, innocently fancying that he, also, might feel the need of a companion with whom to talk over the brilliant passages of the night. And a moment ensued when she debated taking his hand. She was too soon glad that her intuition forbade the demonstration.

"It was all so beautiful, papa," she said, timidly. "I have no way to tell you how I thank you."

"You may do that," he replied, evenly, with no unkindness, with no kindness, either, in the level of his tone, "by never dancing again more than twice with one man in one evening."

"I think I should much prefer not, myself," she returned, lifting her head to face him gravely. "I believe if I cared to dance more than once with one, I should like to dance all of them with him."

Mr. Carewe frowned. "I trust that you discovered none last

night whom you wished to honor with your entire programme?"

"No," she laughed, "not last night."

Her father tossed away his cigar abruptly "Is it too much to hope," he inquired, "that when you discover a gentleman with whom you desire to waltz all night, you will omit to mention the fact to him?"

There was a brief flash of her eye as she recalled her impulse to take his hand, but she immediately looked at him with such complete seriousness that he feared his irony had been thrown away.

"I'll remember not to mention it," she answered. "I'll tell him you told me not too."

"I think you may retire now," said Mr. Carewe, sharply.

She rose from the steps, went to the door, then turned at the threshold. "Were all your friends here, papa?"

"Do you think that every ninny who gabbled in my house last night was my friend?" he said, angrily. "There was one friend of mine, Mrs. Tanberry, who wasn't here, because she is out of town; but I do not imagine that you are inquiring about women. You mean: Was every unmarried male idiot who could afford a swallow-tailed coat and a clean pair of gloves cavorting about the place? Yes, miss, they were all here except two, and one of those is a fool, the other a knave."

"Can't I know the fool?" she asked, eagerly.

"I rejoice to find them so rare in your experience!" he

retorted. "This one is out of town, though I have no doubt you will see him sufficiently often when be returns. His name is Crailey Gray, and he is to marry Fanchon Bareaud— if he remembers!"

"And the knave?"

"Is one!" Carewe shut his teeth with a venomous snap, and his whole face reddened suddenly. "I'll mention this fellow once—now," he said, speaking each word with emphasis. "His name is Vanrevel. You see that gate; you see the line of my property there: the man himself, as well as every other person in the town, remembers well that the last time I spoke to him, it was to tell him that if he ever set foot on ground of mine I'd shoot him down, and he knows, and they all know, I shall keep my word! Elsewhere, I told him that for the sake of public peace, I should ignore him. I do. You will see him everywhere; but it will not be difficult; no one will have the hardihood to present him to my daughter. The quarrel between us—" Mr. Carewe broke off for a moment, his hands clinching the arms of his chair, while he swallowed with difficulty, as though he choked upon some acrid bolus, and he was so strongly agitated by his own mention of his enemy that he controlled himself by a painful effort of his will. "The quarrel between us is political—and personal. You will remember."

"I shall remember," she answered in a rather frightened voice.

. . . It was long before she fell asleep. "I alone must hover about the gates or steal into your garden like a thief," the Incroyable had said. "The last time I spoke to him it was to tell him that if he ever set foot on ground of mine, I'd shoot him down! " had been her father's declaration. And Mr. Carewe had spoken with the most undeniable air of meaning what he said. Yet she knew that the Incroyable would come again.

Also, with hot cheeks pressed into her pillow, Miss Betty had identified the young man in the white hat, that dark person whose hand she had far too impetuously seized in both of hers. Aha! It was this gentleman who looked into people's eyes and stammered so sincerely over a pretty speech that you almost believed him, it was he who was to marry Fanchon Bareaud—" if he remembers!" No wonder Fanchon had been in such a hurry to get him away . . . . "If he remembers!" Such was that young man's character, was it? Miss Carewe laughed aloud to her pillow: for, was one to guess the reason, also, of his not having come to her ball? Had the poor man been commanded to be "out of town?"

Then, remembering the piquant and generous face of Fanchon, Betty clinched her fingers tightly and crushed the imp who had suggested the unworthy thought, crushed him to a wretched pulp and threw him out of the open window. He immediately sneaked in by the back way, for, in spite of her victory, she still felt a little sorry for poor Fanchon.

CHAPTER IV

"BUT SPARE YOUR COUNTRY'S FLAG"

If it be true that love is the great incentive to the useless arts, the number of gentlemen who became poets for the sake of Miss Betty Carewe need not be considered extraordinary. Of all that was written of her dancing, Tom Vanrevel's lines, "I Danced with Her beneath the Lights" (which he certainly had not done when he wrote them) were, perhaps, next to Crailey Gray's in merit, though Tom burned his rhymes after reading them to Crailey. Other troubadours were not so modest, and the Rouen Journal found no lack of tuneful offering, that spring, generously printing all of it, even at the period when it became epidemic. The public had little difficulty in recognizing the work of Mr. Francis Chenoweth in an anonymous "Sonnet" (of twenty-three lines) which appeared in the issue following Miss Carewe's debut. Mr. Chenoweth wrote that while dancing the mazourka with a Lovely Being, the sweetest feelings of his soul, in a celestial stream, bore him away beyond control, in a seraphic dream; and he untruthfully stated that at the same time he saw her wipe the silent tear, omitting, however, to venture any explanation of the cause of her emotion. Old General Trumble boldly signed his poem in full. It was called "An Ode upon Miss C—'s Waltzing," and it began:

"When Bettina found fair Rouen's shore, And her aged father to us bore Her from the cloister neat, She waltzed upon the ball-room floor, And lightly twirled upon her feet."

Mr. Carewe was rightfully indignant, and refused to acknowledge the General's salutation at their next meeting: Trumble was fifteen years older than he.

As Crailey Gray never danced with Miss Carewe, it is somewhat singular that she should have been the inspiration of his swinging verses in waltz measure, "Heart-strings on a Violin," the sense of which was that when a violin had played for her dancing, the instrument should be shattered as wine-glasses are after a great toast. However, no one, except the author himself, knew that Betty was the subject; for Crailey certainly did not mention it to Miss Bareaud, nor to his best friend, Vanrevel.

It was to some degree a strange comradeship between these two young men; their tastes led them so often in opposite directions. They had rooms together over their offices in the "Madrillon Block" on Main Street, and the lights shone late from their windows every night in the year. Sometimes that would mean only that the two friends were talking, for they never reached a silent intimacy, but, even after several years of companionship, were rarely seen together when not in interested, often eager, conversation, so that people wondered what in the world they still found to say to each other. But many a night the late-shining lamp meant that Tom sat alone, with a brief or a book, or wooed the long hours with his magical guitar. For he never went to bed until the other came home.

And if daylight came without Crailey, Vanrevel would go out, yawning mightily, to look for him; and when there was no finding him, Tom would come back, sleepless, to the day's work. Crailey was called "peculiar" and he explained, with a kind of jovial helplessness, that he was always prepared for the unexpected in himself, nor did such a view detract from his picturesqueness to his own perusal of himself; though it was not only to himself that he was interesting. To the vision of the lookers-on in Rouen, quiet souls who hovered along the walls at merry-makings and cheerfully counted themselves spectators at the play, Crailey Gray held the centre of the stage and was the chief comedian of the place. Wit, poet, and scapegrace, the small society sometimes seemed the mere background set for his performances, spectacles which he, also, enjoyed, and from the best seat in the house; for he was not content as the actor, but must be the Prince in the box as well.

His friendship for Tom Vanrevel was, in a measure, that of the vine for the oak. He was full of levities at Tom's expense, which the other bore with a grin of sympathetic compre- hension, or, at long intervals, returned upon Crailey with devastating effect. Vanrevel was the one steadying thing in his life, and, at the same time, the only one of the young men upon whom he did not have an almost mesmeric influence. In good truth, Crailey was the ringleader in all the devilries of the town. Many a youth swore to avoid the roisterer's company for all time, and, within two hours of the vow, found himself, flagon in hand, engaged in a bout that would last the night, with Mr. Gray out-bumpering the hardiest, at the head of the table. And, the next morning, the fevered, scarlet-eyed perjurer might creep shaking to his wretched tasks, only to behold the cause of his folly and headache tripping merrily along the street, smiling, clean-shaven, and fresh as a dew-born primrose, with, perchance, two or three of the prettiest girls in town at his elbow to greet his sallies with approving laughter.

Crailey had been so long in the habit of following every

impulse, no matter how mad, that he enjoyed an almost perfect immunity from condemnation, and, whatever his deeds, Rouen had learned to say, with a chuckle, that it was "only Crailey Gray again." But his followers were not so privileged. Thus, when Mr. Gray, who in his libations sometimes developed the humor of an urchin, went to the Pound at three in the morning of New Year's Day, hung sleigh-bells about the necks of the cattle and drove them up and down the streets, himself hideously blowing a bass horn from the back of a big brown steer, those roused from slumber ceased to rage, and accepted the exploit as a rare joke, on learning that it was "only Crailey Gray;" but the unfortunate young Chenoweth was heavily frowned upon and properly upbraided because he had followed in the wake of the bovine procession, mildly attempting to play upon a flageolet.

Crailey never denied a folly nor defended an escapade. The latter was always done for him, because he talked of his "graceless misdoings" (so he was wont, smilingly, to call them) over cups of tea in the afternoons with old ladies, lamenting, in his musical voice, the lack of female relatives to guide him. He was charmingly attentive to the elderly women, not from policy, but because his manner was uncontrollably chivalrous; and, ever a gallant listener, were the speaker young, old, great or humble, he never forgot to catch the last words of a sentence, and seldom suffered for a reply, even when he had drowsed through a question. Moreover, no one ever heard him speak a sullen word, nor saw him wear a brow of depression. The single creed to which he was constant was that of good cheer; he was the very apostle of gayety, preaching it in parlor and bar; and made merry friends with battered tramps and homeless dogs in the streets at night.

Now and then he would spend several days in the offices of

Gray & Vanrevel, Attorneys and Counsellors-at-Law, wearing an air of unassailable virtue; though he did not far overstate the case when he said, "Tom does all the work and gives me all the money not to bother him when he's getting up a case."

The working member of the firm got up cases to notable effect, and few lawyers in the State enjoyed having Tom Vanrevel on the other side. There was nothing about him of the floridity prevalent at that time; he withered "oratory" before the court; he was the foe of jury pathos; and, despising noise and the habitual voice-dip at the end of a sentence, was, nevertheless, at times an almost fearfully effective orator. So, by degrees the firm of Gray & Vanrevel, young as it was, and in spite of the idle apprentice, had grown to be the most prosperous in the district. For this eminence Crailey was never accused of assuming the credit. Nor did he ever miss an opportunity of making known how much he owed to his partner. What he owed, in brief, was everything. How well Vanrevel worked was demonstrated every day, but how hard he worked, only Crailey knew. The latter had grown to depend upon him for even his political beliefs, and lightly followed his partner into Abolitionism; though that was to risk unpopularity, bitter hatred, and worse. Fortunately, on certain occasions, Vanrevel had made himself (if not his creed) respected, at least so far that there was no longer danger of mob-violence for an Abolitionist in Rouen. He was a cool-headed young man ordinarily, and possessed of an elusive forcefulness not to be trifled with, though he was a quiet man, and had what they called a "fine manner." And, not in the latter, but in his dress, there was an echo of the Beau, which afforded Mr. Gray a point of attack for sallies of wit; there was a touch of the dandy about Vanrevel; he had a large and versatile wardrobe, and his clothes always fit him not only in line but in color; even women saw how nobly they were fashioned.

These two young men were members of a cheerful band, who feasted, laughed, wrangled over politics, danced, made love, and sang terrible chords on summer evenings, together, as young men will. Will Cummings, editor of the Rouen Journal, was one of these; a tall, sallow man, very thin, very awkward and very gentle. Mr. Cummings proved himself always ready with a loud and friendly laugh for the poorest joke in the world, his countenance shining with such kindness that no one ever had the heart to reproach him with the evils of his journalistic performances, or for the things he broke when he danced. Another was Tappingham Marsh, an exceedingly handsome person, somewhat languid in appearance, dainty in manner with women, offhand with men; almost as reckless as Crailey, and often the latter's companion and assistant in dissipation. Young Francis Chenoweth never failed to follow both into whatever they planned; he was short and pink, and the uptilt of his nose was coherent with the appealing earnestness which was habitual with him. Eugene Madrillon was the sixth of these intimates; a dark man, whose Latin eyes and color advertised his French ancestry as plainly as his emotionless mouth and lack of gesture betrayed the mingling of another strain.

All these, and others of the town, were wont to "talk politics" a great deal at the little club on Main Street and all were apt to fall foul of Tom Vanrevel or Crailey Gray before the end of any discussion. For those were the days when they twisted the Lion's tail in vehement and bitter earnest; when the eagle screamed in mixed figures; when few men knew how to talk, and many orated; when party strife was savagely personal; when intolerance was called the "pure fire of patriotism;" when criticism of the existing order of things surely incurred fiery anathema and black invective; and brave was he, indeed, who dared to hint that his country, as a whole and politically, did lack some two or three particular virtues, and that the first step toward obtaining them would be to help it to realize their absence.

This latter point-of-view was that of the firm of Gray & Vanrevel, which was a unit in such matters. Crailey did most of the talking—quite beautifully, too—and both had to stand against odds in many a sour argument, for they were not only Abolitionists, but opposed the attitude of their country in its difficulty with Mexico; and, in common with other men of the time who took their stand, they had to grow accustomed to being called Disloyal Traitors, Foreign Toadies, Malignants, and Traducers of the Flag. Tom had long been used to epithets of this sort, suffering their sting in quiet, and was glad when he could keep Crailey out of worse employment than standing firm for an unpopular belief.

There was one place to which Vanrevel, seeking his friend and partner, when the latter did not come home at night, could not go; this was the Tower Chamber, and it was in that mysterious apartment of the Carewe cupola that Crailey was apt to be deeply occupied when he remained away until daylight. Strange as it appears, Mr. Gray maintained peculiar relations of intimacy with Robert Carewe, in spite of the feud between Carewe and his own best friend. This intimacy, which did not necessarily imply any mutual fondness (though Crailey seemed to dislike nobody), was betokened by a furtive understanding, of a sort, between them. They held brief, earnest conversations on the street, or in corners when they met at other people's houses, always speaking in voices too low to be overheard; and they exercised a mysterious symbolism, somewhat in the manner of fellow members of a secret society: they had been observed to communicate across crowded rooms, by lifted eyebrow, nod of head, or a surreptitious turn of the wrist: so that those who observed them knew that a question had been asked and answered.

It was noticed, also, that there were five other initiates to this masonry: Eugene Madrillon, the elder Chenoweth, General Trumble, Tappingham Marsh, and Jefferson Bareaud. Thus, on the afternoon following Miss Betty's introduction to Rouen's favorite sons and daughters, Mr. Carewe, driving down Main Street, held up one forefinger to Madrillon as he saw the young man turning in at the club. Eugene nodded gravely, and, as he went in, discovering Marsh, the General, and others, listening to Mr. Gray's explanation of his return from the river with no fish, stealthily held up one finger in his turn. Trumble replied with a wink, Tappingham nodded, but Crailey slightly shook his head. Marsh and the General started with surprise, and stared incredulously. That Crailey should shake his head! If the signal had been for a church-meeting they might have understood.

Mr. Gray's conduct was surprising two other people at about the same time: Tom Vanrevel and Fanchon Bareaud; the former by his sudden devotion to the law; the latter by her sudden devotion to herself. In a breath, he became almost a domestic character. No more did he spend his afternoons between the club and the Rouen House bar, nor was his bay mare so often seen stamping down the ground about Mrs. McDougal's hitching-post while McDougal was out on the prairie with his engineering squad. The idle apprentice was at his desk, and in the daytime he displayed an aversion for the streets, which was more than his partner did, for the industrious Tom, undergoing quite as remarkable an alteration of habit, became, all at once, little better than a corner-loafer. His favorite lounging-place was a small drug-store where Carewe Street debouched upon Main; nevertheless, so adhesive is a reputation once fastened, his air of being there upon business deceived everyone except Mr. Gray.

Miss Bareaud was even happier than she was astonished (and she was mightily astonished) to find her betrothed developing a taste for her society alone. Formerly, she had counted upon the gayeties of her home to keep Crailey near her; now, however, he told her tenderly he wished to have her all to himself. This was not like him, but Fanchon did not question; and it was very sweet to her that be began to make it his custom to come in by a side gate and meet her under an apple-tree in the dusk, where they would sit quietly together through the evening, listening to the noise and laughter from the lighted house.

That house was the most hospitable in Rouen. Always cheerfully "full of company," as they said, it was the sort of house where a carpet-dance could be arranged in half an hour; a house with a sideboard like the widow's cruse; the young men always found more. Mrs. Bareaud, a Southerner, loving to persuade the visitor that her home was his, not hers, lived only for her art, which was that of the table. Evil cooks, taking service with her, became virtuous, dealt with nectar and ambrosia, and grew fit to pander to Olympus, learning of their mistress secrets to make the ill-disposed as genial gods ere they departed. Mr. Bareaud at fifty had lived so well that he gave up walking, which did not trouble him; but at sixty he gave up dancing, which did trouble him. His only hope, he declared, was in Crailey Gray's promise to invent for him: a concave partner.

There was a thin, quizzing shank of a son, Jefferson, who lived upon quinine, ague and deviltry; and there were the two daughters, Fanchon and Virginia. The latter was three years older than Fanchon, as dark as Fanchon was fair, though not nearly so pretty: a small, good-natured, romping sprite of a girl, who had handed down the heart and hand of Crailey Gray to her sister with the best grace in the world. For she had been the heroine of one of Mr. Gray's half-dozen or so most serious affairs, and, after a furious rivalry with Mr. Carewe, the victory was generally conceded to Crailey. His triumph had been of about a fort-night's duration when Fanchon returned from St. Mary's; and, with the advent of the younger sister, the elder, who had decided that Crailey was the incomparable she had dreamed of since infancy, was generously allowed to discover that he was not that vision— that she had fallen in love with her own idea of him; whereas Fanchon cared only that he be Crailey Gray, whatever kind of vision that was. And Fanchon discovered that it was a great many kinds.

The transfer was made comfortably, with nice judgment of a respectable interregnum, and to the greater happiness of each of the three young people; no objection ensuing from the easy-going parents, who were devotedly fond of Crailey, while the town laughed and said it was only that absurd Crailey Gray again. He and Virginia were the best of friends, and accepted their new relation with a preposterous lack of embarrassment.

To be in love with Crailey became Fanchon's vocation; she spent all her time at it, and produced a blurred effect upon strangers. The only man with whom she seemed quite alive was Vanrevel: a little because Tom talked of Crailey, and a great deal because she could talk of Crailey to Tom; could tell him freely, as she could tell no one else, how wonderful Crailey was, and explain to him her lover's vagaries on the ground that it was a necessity of geniuses to be unlike the less gifted. Nor was she alone in suspecting Mr. Gray of genius: in the first place, he was so odd; in the second, his poems were "already attracting more than local attention," as the Journal remarked, generously, for Crailey had ceased to present his rhymes to that valuable paper. Ay! Boston, no less, was his mart.

He was rather radical in his literary preferences, and hurt the elder Chenoweth's feelings by laughing heartily at some poems of the late Lord Byron; offended many people by disliking the style of Sir Edward Bulwer, and even refused to admit that James Fenimore Cooper was the greatest novelist that ever lived. But these things were as nothing compared with his unpatriotic defence of Charles Dickens. Many Americans had fallen into a great rage over the vivacious assault upon the United States in "Martin Chuzzlewit;" nevertheless, Crailey still boldly hailed him (as everyone had heretofore agreed) the most dexterous writer of his day and the most notable humorist of any day. Of course the Englishman had not visited and thoroughly studied such a city as Rouen, Crailey confessed, twinklingly; but, after all, wasn't there some truth in "Martin Chuzzlewit?" Mr. Dickens might have been far from a clear understanding of our people; but didn't it argue a pretty ticklish vanity in ourselves that we were so fiercely resentful of satire; and was not this very heat over "Martin Chuzzlewit" a confirmation of one of the points the book had presented against us? General Trumble replied to this suggestion with a personal one to the effect that a man capable of saying a good word for so monstrous a slander, that a man, sir, capable of declaring his native country to be vain or sensitive ought to be horsewhipped, and at this Crailey laughed consumedly.

Trumble retorted with the names of Benedict Arnold and Aaron Burr. "And if it comes to a war with these Greasers," he spluttered apoplectically, "and it is coming, mighty soon, we'll find Mr. Gray down in Mexico, throwing mud on the Stars and Stripes and cheering for that one-legged horse-thief, Santa Anna! Anything to seek out something foolish amongst your own people!"

"Don't have to seek far, sometimes, General," murmured Crailey, from the depths of the best chair in the club, whereupon Trumble, not trusting himself to answer, went out to the street.

And yet, before that same evening was over, the General had shed honest tears of admiration and pity for Crailey Gray; and Miss Betty saw her Incroyable again, for that night (the second after the Carewe dance) Rouen beheld the great warehouse fire.

CHAPTER V

NERO NOT THE LAST VIOLINIST OF HIS KIND

Miss Carewe was at her desk, writing to Sister Cecilia, whom she most loved of all the world, when the bells startled her with their sudden clangor. The quill dropped from her hand; she started to her feet, wide-eyed, not understanding; while the whole town, drowsing peacefully a moment ago, resounded immediately with a loud confusion. She ran to the front door and looked out, her heart beating wildly.

The western sky was touched with a soft rose-color, which quickly became a warm glow, fluctuated, and, in the instant, shot up like the coming of a full Aurora. Then through the broken foliage of the treetops could be seen the orange curls of flames, three-quarters of a mile away though they were.

People, calling loudly that "it was Carewe's warehouses," were running down the street. From the stable, old Nelson, on her father's best horse, came galloping, and seeing the white figure in the doorway, cried out in a quavering voice, without checking his steed.

"I goin' tell yo' pa, Miss Betty, he in de kentry on lan' bus'ness. Go back in de house, Missy!"

The other servants, like ragged sketches in the night, flitted by, with excited ejaculations, to join the runners, and Miss Betty followed them across the dew-strewn turf in her night slippers, but at the gate she stopped.

From up the street came the sound of a bell smaller than those of the churches and courthouse, yet one that outdid all others in the madness of its appeal to clear the way. It was borne along by what seemed at first an indefinite black mass, but which—as the Aurora grew keener, producing even here a faint, yellow twilight—resolved itself into a mob of hoarsely-shouting men and boys, who were running and tugging at ropes, which drew along three extraordinary vehicles. They came rapidly down the street and passed Miss Betty with a hubbub and din beyond all understanding; one line of men, most of them in red shirts and oil-cloth helmets, at a dead run with the hose-cart; a second line with the hand-engine; the third dragging the ladder-wagon. One man was riding, a tall, straight gentleman in evening clothes and without a hat, who stood precariously in the hose-cart, calling in an annoyed tone through a brazen trumpet. Miss Betty recognized him at once; it was he who caught her kitten; and she thought that if she bad been Fanchon Bareaud she must have screamed a warning, for his balance appeared a thing of mere luck, and, if he fell, he would be trampled under foot and probably run over by the engine. But, happily (she remembered), she was not Fanchon Bareaud!

Before, behind, and beside the Department, raced a throng of boys, wild with the joy experienced by their species when property is being handsomely destroyed; after them came panting women, holding their sides and gasping with the effort to keep up with the flying procession.

Miss Betty trembled, for she had never seen the like in her life; she stood close to the hedge and let them go by; then she turned in after them and ran like a fleet young deer. She was going to the fire.

Over all the uproar could be heard the angry voice through the trumpet, calling the turns of the streets to the men in the van, upbraiding them and those of the other two companies impartially; and few of his hearers denied the chief his right to express some chagrin; since the Department (organized a half-year, hard-drilled, and this its first fire worth the name) was late on account of the refusal of the members to move until they had donned their new uniforms; for the uniforms had arrived from Philadelphia two months ago, and tonight offered the first opportunity to display them in public.

"Hail Vanrevel!" panted Tappingham Marsh to Eugene Madrillon, as the two, running in the van of the "Hose Company," splattered through a mud-puddle. "You'd think he was Carewe's only son and heir instead of his worst enemy. Hark to the man!"

"I'd let it burn, if I were he," returned the other.

"It was all Crailey's fault," said Tappingham, swinging an arm free to wipe the spattered mud from his face. "He swore he wouldn't budge without his uniform, and the rest only backed him up; that was all. Crailey said Carewe could better afford to lose his shanties than the overworked Department its first chance to look beautiful and earnest. Tom asked him why he didn't send for a fiddle," Marsh finished with a chuckle.

"Carewe might afford to lose a little, even a warehouse or two, if only out of what he's taken from Crailey and the rest of us, these three years!"

"Taken from Vanrevel, you mean. Who doesn't know where

Crailey's—Here's Main Street; look out for the turn!"

They swung out of the thick shadows of Carewe Street into full view of the fire, and their faces were illuminated as by sunrise.

The warehouses stood on the river-bank, at the foot of the street, just south of the new "covered bridge." There were four of them, huge, bare-sided buildings; the two nearer the bridge of brick, the others of wood, and all of them rich with stores of every kind of river-merchandise and costly freight: furniture that had voyaged from New England down the long coast, across the Mexican Gulf, through the flat Delta, and had made the winding journey up the great river a thousand miles, and almost a thousand more, following the greater and lesser tributaries; cloth from Connecticut that had been sold in Philadelphia, then carried over mountains and through forests by steam, by canal, by stage, and six-mule freight-wagons, to Pittsburg, down the Ohio, and thence up to Rouen on the packet; Tennessee cotton, on its way to Massachusetts and Rhode Island spindles, lay there beside huge mounds of raw wool from Illinois, ready to be fed to the Rouen mill; dates and nuts from the Caribbean Sea; lemons from groves of the faraway tropics; cigars from the Antilles; tobacco from Virginia and Kentucky; most precious of all, the great granary of the farmers' wheat from the level fields at home; and all the rich stores and the houses that held them, as well as the wharves upon which they had been landed, and the steamers that brought them up the Rouen River, belonged to Robert Carewe.

That it was her father's property which was imperilled attested to the justification of Miss Betty in running to a fire; and, as she followed the crowd into Main Street, she felt a not unpleasant proprietary interest in the spectacle. Very opposite sensations animated the breast of the man with the trumpet, who was more acutely conscious than any other that these were Robert Carewe's possessions which were burning so handsomely. Nor was he the only one among the firemen who ground his teeth over the folly of the uniforms; for now they could plainly see the ruin being wrought, the devastation threatened. The two upper stories of the southernmost warehouse had swathed themselves in one great flame; the building next on the north, also of frame, was smoking heavily; and there was a wind from the southwest, which, continuing with the fire unchecked, threatened the town itself. There was work for the Volunteer Brigade that night.

They came down Main Street with a rush, the figure of their chief swaying over them on his high perch, while their shouting was drowned in the louder roar of greeting from the crowd, into which they plunged as a diver into the water, swirls and eddies of people marking the wake. A moment later a section of the roof of the burning warehouse fell in, with a sonorous and reverberating crash.

The "Engine Company" ran the force-pump out to the end of one of the lower wharves; two lines of pipe were attached; two rows of men mounted the planks for the pumpers, and, at the word of command, began the up-and-down of the hand-machine with admirable vim. Nothing happened; the water did not come; something appeared to be wrong with the mechanism. As everyone felt the crucial need of haste, nothing could have been more natural than that all the members of the "Engine Company" should simultaneously endeavor to repair the defect; therefore ensued upon the spot a species of riot which put the engine out of its sphere of usefulness.

In the meantime, fifty or sixty men and boys who ran with the machines, but who had no place in their operation, being the Bucket Brigade, had formed a line and were throwing large pails of water in the general direction of the southern-most warehouse, which it was now impossible to save; while the gentlemen of the "Hook-and-Ladder Company," abandoning their wagons, and armed with axes, heroically assaulted the big door of the granary, the second building, whence they were driven by the exasperated chief, who informed them that the only way to save the wheat was to save the building. Crailey Gray, one of the berated axemen, remained by the shattered door after the others had gone, and, struck by a sudden thought, set his hand upon the iron latch and opened the door by this simple process. It was not locked. Crailey leaned against the casement and laughed with his whole soul and body.

Meanwhile, by dint of shouting in men's ears when near them, through the trumpet when distant, tearing axes from their hands, imperiously gesticulating to subordinate commanders, and lingering in no one spot for more than a second, Mr. Vanrevel reduced his forces to a semblance of order in a remarkably short time, considering the confusion into which they had fallen.

The space between the burning warehouse and that next it was not more than fifty feet in width, but fifty feet so hot no one took thought of entering there; an area as discomfiting in appearance as it was beautiful with the thick rain of sparks and firebrands that fell upon it. But the chief had decided that this space must be occupied, and more: must be held, since it was the only point of defence for the second warehouse. The roof of this building would burn, which would mean the destruction of the warehouse, unless it could be mounted, because the streams of water could not play upon it from the ground, nor, from the ladders, do much more than wet the projecting eaves. It was a gable roof, the eaves twenty feet lower on the south side than on the north, where the ladders could not hope to reach them. Vanrevel swung his line of bucketeers round to throw water, not upon the flames, but upon the ladder-men.

Miss Carewe stood in the crowd upon the opposite side of the broad street. Even there her cheeks were uncomfortably hot, and sometimes she had to brush a spark from her shoulder, though she was too much excited to mind this. She was watching the beautiful fiery furnace between the north wall of the burning warehouse and the south wall of its neighbor, the fifty feet brilliant and misty with vaporous rose-color, dotted with the myriad red stars, her eyes shining with the reflection of their fierce beauty. She saw how the vapors moved there, like men walking in fire, and she was vaguely recalling Shadrach, Meshach, and Abed-nego, when, over the silhouetted heads of the crowd before her, a long black ladder rose, wobbled, tilted crazily, then lamely advanced and ranged itself against the south wall of the second warehouse, its top rung striking ten feet short of the eaves. She hoped that no one had any notion of mounting that ladder.

A figure appeared upon it immediately, that of a gentleman, bareheaded and in evening dress, with a brass trumpet swinging from a cord about his shoulders; the noise grew less; the shouting died away, and the crowd became almost silent, as the figure, climbing slowly drew up above their heads. Two or three rungs beneath, came a second—a man in helmet and uniform. The clothes of both men, drenched by the bucketeers, clung to them, steaming. As the second figure mounted, a third appeared; but this was the last, for the ladder was frail, and sagged toward the smoking wall with the weight of the three.

The chief, three-fourths of the way to the top, shouted down a stifled command, and a short grappling-ladder, fitted at one end with a pair of spiked iron hooks, was passed to him.

Then he toiled upward until his feet rested on the third rung from the top; here he turned, setting his back to the wall, lifted the grappling-ladder high over his head so that it rested against the eaves above him, and brought it down sharply, fastening the spiked hooks in the roof. As the eaves projected fully three feet, this left the grappling-ladder hanging that distance out from the wall, its lowest rung a little above the level of the chief's shoulders.

Miss Betty drew in her breath with a little choked cry. There was a small terraced hill of piled-up packing-boxes near her, possession of which had been taken by a company of raggamuffinish boys, and she found herself standing on the highest box and sharing the summit with these questionable youths, almost without noting her action in mounting thither, so strained was the concentration of her attention upon the figure high up in the rose-glow against the warehouse wall. The man, surely, surely, was not going to trust himself to that bit of wooden web hanging from the roof! Where was Miss Bareaud that she permitted it? Ah, if Betty had been Fanchon and madwoman enough to have accepted this madman, she would have compelled him to come down at once, and thereafter would lock him up in the house whenever the bells rang!

But the roof was to be mounted or Robert Carewe's property lost. Already little flames were dancing up from the shingles, where firebrands had fallen, their number increasing with each second. So Vanrevel raised his arms, took a hard grip upon the lowest rung of the grappling-ladder and tried it with his weight; the iron hooks bit deeper into the roof; they held. He swung himself out into the air with nothing beneath him, caught the rung under his knee, and for a moment hung there while the crowd withheld from breathing; then a cloud of smoke, swirling that way, made him the mere ghostly nucleus of himself, blotted him out altogether, and, as it rose slowly upward, showed the ladder free and empty, so that at first there was an instant when they thought that he had fallen. But, as the smoke cleared, there was the tall figure on the roof.

It was an agile and daring thing to do, and the man who did it was mightily applauded. The cheering bothered him, however, for he was trying to make them understand, below, what would happen to the "Engine Company" in case the water was not sent through the lines directly; and what he said should be done to the engineers included things that would have blanched the cheek of the most inventive Spanish Inquisitor that ever lived.

Miss Betty made a gesture as if to a person within whispering distance. "Your coat is on fire," she said in an ordinary conversational tone, without knowing she had spoken aloud, and Mr. Vanrevel, more than one hundred feet away, seemed particularly conscious of the pertinence of her remark. He removed the garment with alacrity, and, for the lack of the tardy water, began to use it as a flail upon the firebrands and little flames about him; the sheer desperate best of a man in a rage, doing what he could when others failed him. Showers of sparks fell upon him; the smoke was rising everywhere from the roof and the walls below; and, growing denser and denser, shrouded him in heavy veils, so that, as he ran hither and thither, now visible, now unseen, stamping and beating and sweeping away the brands that fell, he seemed but the red and ghostly caricature of a Xerxes, ineffectually lashing the sea. They were calling to him imploringly to come down, in heaven's name to come down!

The second man had followed to the top of the ladder against the wall, and there he paused, waiting to pass up the line of hose when the word should come that the force-pump had been repaired; but the people thought that he waited because he was afraid to trust himself to the grappling-ladder. He was afraid, exceedingly afraid; though that was not why he waited; and he was still chuckling over the assault of the axes.

His situation had not much the advantage of that of the chief: his red shirt might have been set with orange jewels, so studded it was with the flying sparks; and, a large brand dropping upon his helmet, he threw up his hand to dislodge it and lost the helmet. The great light fell upon his fair hair and smiling face, and it was then that Miss Betty recognized the Incroyable of her garden.

CHAPTER VI

THE EVER UNPRACTICAL FEMININE

It was an investigating negro child of tender years, who, possessed of a petty sense of cause and effect, brought an illuminative simplicity to bear upon the problem of the force-pump; and a multitudinous agitation greeted his discovery that the engineers had forgotten to connect their pipes with the river.

This naïve omission was fatal to the second warehouse; the wall burst into flame below Crailey Gray, who clung to the top of the ladder, choking, stifled, and dizzily fighting the sparks that covered him, yet still clutching the nozzle of the hose-line they had passed to him. When the stream at last leaped forth, making the nozzle fight in his grasp, he sent it straight up into the air and let the cataract fall back upon himself and upon the two men beneath him on the ladder.

There came a moment of blessed relief; and he looked out over the broad rosy blur of faces in the street, where no one wondered more than he how the water was to reach the roof. Suddenly he started, wiped his eyes with his wet sleeve, and peered intently down from under the shading arm. His roving glance crossed the smoke and flame to rest upon a tall, white figure that stood, full-length above the heads of the people, upon a pedestal wrought with the grotesque images of boys: a girl's figure, still as noon, enrapt, like the statue of some young goddess for whom were made these sacrificial pyres. Mr. Gray recognized his opportunity.

A blackened and unrecognizable face peered down from the eaves, and the voice belonging to it said, angrily: "Why didn't they send up that line before they put the water through it?"

"Never mind, Tom," answered Crailey cheerfully, "I'll bring it up." "You can't; I'll come down for it. Don't be every kind of a fool!"

"You want a monopoly, do you?" And Crailey, calling to Tappingham Marsh, next below him, to come higher, left the writhing nozzle in the latter's possession, swung himself out upon the grappling-ladder, imitating the chief's gymnastics, and immediately, one hand grasping the second rung, one knee crooked over the lowest, leaned head down and took the nozzle from Marsh. It was a heavy weight, and though Marsh supported the line beneath it, the great stream hurtling forth made it a difficult thing to manage, for it wriggled, recoiled and struggled as if it had been alive. Crailey made three attempts to draw himself up; but the strain was too much for his grip, and on the third attempt his fingers melted from the rung, and he swung down fearfully, hanging by his knee, but still clinging to the nozzle.

"Give it up, Crailey; it isn't worth it," Vanrevel called from overhead, not daring the weight of both on the light grappling-ladder.

But though Crailey cared no more for the saving of Robert Carewe's property than for a butterfly's wing in China, he could not give up now, any more than as a lad be could have forborne to turn somersaults when the prettiest little girl looked out of the school-house window. He passed the nozzle to Tappingham, caught the second rung with his left hand, and, once more hanging head downward, seized the nozzle; then, with his knee hooked tight, as the gushing water described a huge semicircle upon the smoke and hot vapor, he made a mad lurch through the air, while women shrieked; but he landed upright, half-sitting on the lowest rung. He climbed the grappling-ladder swiftly, in spite of the weight and contortions of the unmanageable beast he carried with him; Tom leaned far down and took it from him; and Crailey, passing the eaves, fell, exhausted, upon the roof. Just as he reached this temporary security, a lady was borne, fainting, out of the acclaiming crowd. Fanchon was there.

Word had been passed to the gentlemen of the "Engine Company" to shut off the water in order to allow the line to be carried up the ladder, and they received the command at the moment Tom lifted the nozzle, so that the stream dried up in his hands. This was the last straw, and the blackened, singed and scarred chief, setting the trumpet to his lips, gave himself entirely to wrath.

It struck Crailey, even as be lay, coughing and weeping with smoke, that there was something splendid and large in the other's rage. Vanrevel was ordinarily so steady and cool that this was worth seeing, this berserker gesture; worth hearing, this wonderful profanity, like Washington's one fit of cursing; and Crailey, knowing Tom, knew, too, that it had not come upon him because Carewe had a daughter into whose eyes Tom had looked; nor did he rage because he believed that Crailey's life and his were in the greater hazard for the lack of every drop of water that should have issued from the empty nozzle. Their lungs were burdened with smoke, while the intolerable smarting of throat, eyes, and nostrils was like the incision of a thousand needles in the membranes; their clothes were luminous with glowing circles where the sparks were eating; the blaze widened on the wall beneath them, and Marsh was shouting hoarsely that he could no longer hold his position on the ladder; yet Crailey knew that none of this was in Tom's mind as he stood, scorched, blistered, and haggard, on the edge of the roof, shaking his fist at the world. It was because his chance of saving the property of a man he despised was being endangered.

Crailey stretched forth a hand and touched his friend's knee. "Your side of the conversation is a trifle loud, Tom," he said. "Miss Carewe is down there, across the street, on a pile of boxes."

Tom stopped in the middle of a word, for which he may have received but half a black stroke from the recording angel. He wheeled toward the street, and, shielding his inflamed eyes with his hand, gazed downward in a stricken silence. From that moment Mr. Vanrevel's instructions to his followers were of a decorum at which not the meekest Sunday-school scholar dare have cavilled.

The three men now on the long ladder, Marsh, Eugene Madrillon, and Will Cummings, found their position untenable; for the flames, reaching all along the wall, were licking at the ladder itself, between Marsh and Eugene. "I can't stand this any longer," gasped Tappingham, "but I can't leave those two up there, either."

"Not alone," shouted Cummings from beneath Madrillon. "Let's go up."

Thus it happened, that when the water came again, and Vanrevel let it fall in a grateful cascade upon Crailey and himself, three manly voices were heard singing, as three men toiled through the billows of rosy gray, below the beleaguered pair:

"Oh the noble Duke of York, He had Ten thousand men; He marched them up the side of a house, And marched them down again!"

A head appeared above the eaves, and Marsh, then Eugene, then Cummings, came crawling over the cornice in turn, to join their comrades. They were a gallant band, those young gentlemen of Rouen, and they came with the ironical song on their lips, and, looking at one another, ragged and scarified, burst into hoarse but indomitable laughter.

Two others made an attempt to follow, and would not be restrained. It was noticed that parts of the lower ladder had been charring; and the ladder-men were preparing to remove it to a less dangerous point, when old General Trumble and young Jefferson Bareaud made a rush to mount it, and were well upon their upward way before the ladder, weakened at the middle, sagged, splintered, and broke, Trumble and Bareaud falling with it. And there was the grappling-ladder, dangling forty feet above the ground; and there were the five upon the roof.

The Department had no other ladder of more than half the length of the shattered one. Not only the Department, but every soul in Rouen, knew that; and there rose the thick, low sigh of a multitude, a sound frightful to hear. It became a groan, then swelled into a deep cry of alarm and lamentation.

And now, almost simultaneously, the west wall of the building, and the south wall, and all the southwestern portions of the roof, covered themselves with voluminous mantles of flame, which increased so hugely and with such savage rapidity that the one stream on the roof was seen to be but a ridiculous and useless opposition.

Everybody began to shout advice to his neighbor; and nobody listened even to himself. The firemen were in as great a turmoil as was the crowd, while women covered their eyes. Young Frank Chenoweth was sobbing curses upon the bruised and shaking Trumble and Jefferson Bareaud, who could only stand remorseful, impotently groaning, and made no answer.

The walls of the southernmost warehouse followed the roof, crashing inward one after the other, a sacrificial pyre with its purpose consummated; and in the seeth and flare of its passing, Tom Vanrevel again shaded his eyes with his hand, and looked down across the upturned faces. The pedestal with the grotesque carvings was still there; but the crowning figure had disappeared—the young goddess was gone. For she, of all that throng, had an idea in her head, and, after screaming it to every man within reach, only to discover the impossibility of making herself understood in that Babel, she was struggling to make her way toward the second ware-house, through the swaying jam of people. It was a difficult task, as the farther in she managed to go, the denser became the press and the more tightly she found the people wedged, until she received involuntary aid from the firemen. In turning their second stream to play ineffectually upon the lower strata of flame, they accidentally deflected it toward the crowd, who separated wildly, leaving a big gap, of which Miss Betty took instant advantage. She darted across, and the next moment, unnoticed, had entered the building through the door which Crailey Gray had opened.

The five young men on the roof were well aware that there was little to do but to wait, and soon they would see which was to win, they or the fire; so they shifted their line of hose to the eastern front of the building—out of harm's way, for a little time, at least—and held the muzzle steady, watching its work. And in truth it was not long before they understood which would conquer. The southern and western portions of the building had flung out great flames that fluttered and flared on the breeze like Titanic flags; and steadily, slowly, at first, then faster as the seconds flew, the five were driven backward, up the low slope of the roof toward the gable-ridge. Tom Vanrevel held the first joint of the nozzle, and he retreated with a sulky face, lifting his foot grudgingly at each step. They were all silent, now, and no one spoke until Will Cummings faltered:

"Surely they'll get a rope up to us some way?"

Will knew as well as did the others that there was no way; but his speech struck the sullen heart of the chief with remorse. He turned. " I hope you'll all forgive me for getting you up here."

A sound, half sob, half giggle, came from the parched lips of Eugene Madrillon, as he patted Tom on the shoulder without speaking, and Crailey nodded quietly, then left the group and went to the eastern edge of the roof and looked out upon the crowd. Cummings dropped the line and sat down, burying his hot face in his arms, for they all saw that Vanrevel thought "it was no use," but a question of a few minutes, and they would retreat across the gable and either jump or go down with the roof.

Since the world began, idle and industrious philosophers have speculated much upon the thoughts of men about to die; yet it cannot be too ingenuous to believe that such thoughts vary as the men, their characters, and conditions of life vary. Nevertheless, pursuant with the traditions of minstrelsy and romance, it is conceivable that young, unmarried men, called upon to face desperate situations, might, at the crucial moment, rush to a common experience of summoning the vision, each of his heart's desire, and to meet, each his doom, with her name upon his lips.

An extraordinary thing occurred in the present instance, for, by means of some fragmentary remarks let fall at the time, and afterward recalled such as Tappingham Marsh's gasping: "At least it will be on her father's roof!" and from other things later overheard, an inevitable deduction has been reached that four of the five gentlemen in the perilous case herein described were occupied with the vision of the same person, to wit: Miss Elizabeth Carewe, "the last—the prettiest—to come to town!"

Crailey Gray, alone, spoke not at all; but why did he strain and strain his eyes toward that empty' pedestal with the grotesque carvings? Did he seek Fanchon there, or was Miss Carewe the last sweet apparition in the fancies of all five of the unhappy young men?

The coincidence of the actual appearance of the lady among them, therefore seemed the more miraculous, when, wan and hopeless, staggering desperately backward to the gable-ridge, they heard a clear contralto voice behind them:

"Hadn't you better all come down now?" it said.—"The stairway will be on fire before long."

Only one thing could have been more shockingly unexpected to the five than that there should be a sixth person on the roof, and this was that the sixth person should be Miss Betty Carewe.

They turned, aghast, agape, chopfallen with astonishment, stunned, and incredulous.

She stood just behind the gable-ridge, smiling amiably, a most incongruous little pink fan in her hand, the smoke-wreaths partly obscuring her and curling between the five and her white dress, like mists floating across the new moon.

Was it but a kindly phantasm of the brain? Was it the incarnation of the last vision of the lost Volunteers? Was it a Valkyrie assuming that lovely likeness to perch upon this eyrie, waiting to bear their heroic souls to Valhalla, or—was it Miss Betty Carewe?

To the chief she spoke—all of them agreed to that afterward—but it was Crailey who answered, while Tom could only stare, and stand wagging his head at the lovely phantom, like a Mandarin on a shelf.

"My mother in heaven!" gasped Crailey. "How did you come up here?"

"There's a trap in the roof on the other side of the ridge," she said, and she began to fan herself with the pink fan. "A stairway runs all the way down—old Nelson showed me through these buildings yesterday—and that side isn't on fire yet. I'm so sorry I didn't think of it until a moment ago, because you could have brought the water up that way. But don't you think you'd better come down now?"

CHAPTER VII

THE COMEDIAN

Not savage Hun, nor "barbarous Vandyke," nor demon Apache, could wish to dwell upon the state of mind of the Chief of the Rouen Volunteer Fire Department; therefore, let the curtain of mercy descend. "Without a word, he turned and dragged the nozzle to the eastern eaves, whence, after a warning gesture to those below, he dropped it to the ground. And, out of compassion, it should be little more than hinted that the gesture of warning was very slight.

When the rescued band reached the foot of the last flight of stairs, they beheld the open doorway as a frame for a great press of intent and contorted faces, every eye still strained to watch the roof; none of the harrowed spectators comprehending the appearance of the girl's figure there, nor able to see whither she had led the five young men, until Tappingham Marsh raised a shout as he leaped out of the door and danced upon the solid earth again.

Then, indeed, there was a mighty uproar; cheer after cheer ascended to the red vault of heaven; women wept, men whooped, and the people rushed for the heroes with wide-open, welcoming arms. Jefferson Bareaud and Frank Chenoweth and General Trumble dashed at Tom Vanrevel with incoherent cries of thanksgiving, shaking his hands and beating him hysterically upon the back. He greeted them with bitter laughter.

"Help get the water into the next warehouse; this one is beyond control, but we can save the other two. Take the lines in through the door!" He brushed the rejoicing friends off abruptly, and went on in a queer, hollow voice: "There are stairs—and I'm so sorry I didn't think of it until a moment ago, because you could have brought the water up that way!"

A remarkable case of desertion had occurred, the previous instant, under his eyes. As the party emerged from the warehouse into the street, Tom heard Crailey say hurriedly to Miss Carewe: "Let me get you away come quickly!" saw him suddenly seize her band, and, eluding the onrushing crowd, run with her round the corner of the building. And somehow, through what inspiration, or through what knowledge of his partner's "temperament," heaven knows, the prophetic soul of the chief was unhappily assured that Crailey would offer himself as escort to her home, and find acceptance. But why not? Was it Crailey who had publicly called his fellow-man fool, idiot, imbecile, at the top of his lungs, only to find himself the proven numskull of the universe! Tom stood for a moment staring after the vanishing pair, while over his face stole the strangest expression that ever man saw there; then, with meekly bowed shoulders, be turned again to his work.

At the corner of the warehouse, Miss Carewe detached her hand from Crailey's, yet still followed him as he made a quick detour round the next building. A minute or two later they found themselves, undetected, upon Main Street in the rear of the crowd. There Crailey paused.

"Forgive me," he said, breathlessly, "for taking your hand. I thought you would like to get away."

She regarded him gravely, so that he found it difficult to read her look, except that it was seriously questioning; but whether the interrogation was addressed to him or to herself he could not determine. After a silence she said:

"I don't know why I followed you. I believe it must have been because you didn't give me time to think."

This, of course, made him even quicker with her than before. "It's all over," he said briskly. "The first warehouse is gone; the second will go, but they'll save the others easily enough, now that you have pointed out that the lines may be utilized otherwise than as adjuncts of performances on the high trapeze!" They were standing by a picket-fence, and he leaned against it, overcome by mirth in which she did not join. Her gravity reacted upon him at once, and his laughter was stopped short. "Will you not accept me as an escort to your home?" he said formally. "I do not know," she returned simply, the sort of honest trouble in her glance that is seen only in very young eyes.

"'What reason in the world!" he returned, with a crafty sharpness of astonishment.

She continued to gaze upon him thoughtfully, while he tried to look into her eyes, but was baffled because the radiant beams from the lady's orbs (as the elder Chenoweth might have said) rested somewhere dangerously near his chin, which worried him, for, though his chin made no retreat and was far from ill-looking, it was, nevertheless, that feature which he most distrusted. "Won't you tell me why not?" he repeated, uneasily.

"Because," she answered at last, speaking hesitatingly, "because it isn't so easy a matter for me as you seem to think. You have not been introduced to me, and I know you never will be, and that what you told me was true."

"Which part of what I told you?" The question escaped from him instantly.

"That the others might come when they liked, but that you could not."

"Oh yes, yes." His expression altered to a sincere dejection; his shoulders drooped, and his voice indicated supreme annoyance. "I might have known someone would tell you! Who was it? Did they say why I—"

"On account of your quarrel with my father."

"My quarrel with your father!" he exclaimed; and his face lit with an elated surprise; his shoulders straightened. He took a step nearer her, and asked, eagerly: "Who told you that?"

"My father himself. He spoke of a Mr. Vanrevel whom he—disliked, and whom I must not meet; and, remembering what you had said, of course I knew that you were he."

"Oh!" Crailey's lips began to form a smile of such appealing and inimitable sweetness that Voltaire would have trusted him; a smile altogether rose-leaves. "Then I lose you," he said, "for my only chance to know you was in keeping it hidden from you. And now you understand!"

"No," she answered, gravely, "I don't understand; that is what troubles me. If I did, and believed you had the right of the difference, I could believe it no sin that you should speak to me, should take me home now. I think it is wrong not to act from your own understanding of things."

The young man set his expression as one indomitably fixed

upon the course of honor, cost what it might; and, in the very action, his lurking pleasure in doing it hopped out in the flicker of a twinkle in his eyes, and as instantly sought cover again—the flea in the rose-jar.

"Then you must ask some other," he said, firmly. "A disinterested person should tell you. The difference was political in the beginning, but became personal afterward; and it is now a quarrel which can never be patched up, though, for my part, I wish that it could be. I can say no more, because a party to it should not speak."

She met his level look squarely at last; and no man ever had a more truthful pair of eyes than Crailey Gray, for it was his great accomplishment that he could adjust his emotion, his reason, and something that might be called his faith, to fit any situation in any character.

"You may take me home," she answered. "I may be wrong, and even disloyal; but I do not feel it so, now. You did a very brave thing tonight to save him from loss, and I think that what you have said was just what you should have said."

So they went down the street, the hubbub and confusion of the fire growing more and more indistinct behind them. They walked slowly, and, for a time, neither spoke; yet the silence was of a kind which the adept rejoiced to have produced thus soon—their second meeting. For he believed there were more strange things in heaven and earth than Horatio wot; and one of the strangest was that whenever he was near an attractive woman during a silence such as this, something not to be defined, but as effective as it was indefinite, always went out from him to her. It was like a word of tenderness, a word too gentle, too compelling, too sweet, to be part of any tongue, spoken or written. And more: this ineffable word had an echo, and came back to him from the woman.

As his partner had in dress, so Crailey had with women, some color of the Beau; but it was not in what experience had given him to recognize as a fact: that they were apt to fall in love with him. (That they were apt to remain in love with him—he understood perfectly—was another matter.) And he knew when they were doing it; could have told them accurately, at each step, what they were feeling, thinking, dreaming, during the process, because he was usually exhibiting the same symptoms to himself at the same time.

Thus, his own breast occupied with that dizzy elation which followed its reception of the insane young god's arrows, and his heart warm with the rise of the old emotion that he knew so well, he was nevertheless able to walk with his finger on the pulse of the exquisite moment, counting her heartbeats and his own.

So, to his fancy, as they walked, the little space between them was hung with brilliant strands, like gossamer chains of gold, already linking them together; every second fixing another slender, precious fetter, binding them closer, drawing her nearer. He waited until they passed into the shadows of the deserted Carewe Street before he spoke. There be stopped abruptly; at which she turned, astonished.

"Now that you have saved my life," he said, in a low, tremulous tone, "what are you going to do with it?"

Her eyes opened almost as widely as they had at her first sight of him in her garden. There was a long pause before she replied, and when she did, it was to his considerable surprise.

"I have never seen a play, except the funny little ones we acted at the convent," she said, "but isn't that the way they speak on the stage?"

Crailey realized that his judgment of the silence bad been mistaken, and yet it was with a thrill of delight that he recognized her clear reading of him. He had been too florid again.

"Let us go." His voice was soft with restrained forgiveness. "You mocked me once before.

"Mocked you?" she repeated, as they went on.

"Mocked me," he said, firmly. "Mocked me for seeming theatrical, and yet you have learned that what I said was true; as you will again."

She mused upon this; then, as in whimsical indulgence to an importunate child:

"Well, tell me what you mean when you say I saved your life."

"You came alone," be began, hastily, "to stand upon that burning roof—"

"Whence all but him had fled!" Her laughter rang out, interrupting him. "My room was on the fourth floor at St. Mary's, and I didn't mind climbing three flights this evening."

Crailey's good-nature was always perfect. "You mock me and you mock me!" he cried, and made her laughter but part of a gay duet. "I know I have gone too fast, have said things I should have waited to say; but, ah! remember the small chance I have against the others who can see you when they like. Don't flout me because I try to make the most of a rare, stolen moment with you."

"Do!" she exclaimed, grave upon the instant. "Do make the most of it! I have nothing but inexperience. Make the most by treating me seriously. Won't you? I know you can, and I—I—" She faltered to a full stop. She was earnest and quiet, and there had been something in her tone, too—as very often there was—that showed how young she was. "Oh!" she began again, turning to him impulsively, "I have thought about you since that evening in the garden, and I have wished I could know you. I can't be quite clear how it happened, but even those few minutes left a number of strong impressions about you. And the strongest was that you were one with whom I could talk of a great many things, if you would only be real with me. I believe—though I'm not sure why I do—that it is very difficult for you to be real; perhaps because you are so different at different times that you aren't sure, yourself, which the real you is. But the person that you are beginning to be for my benefit must be the most trifling of all your selves, lighter and easier to put on than the little mask you carried the other night. If there were nothing better underneath the mask, I might play, too."

"Did you learn this at the convent?" gasped Crailey.

"There was a world there in miniature," she answered, speaking very quickly. "I think all people are made of the same materials, only in such different proportions. I think a little world might hold as much as the largest, if you thought it all out hard enough, and your experience might be just as broad and deep in a small corner of the earth as anywhere else. But I don't know! I want to understand—I want to understand everything! I read books, and there are people—but no one who tells me what I want—I—"

"Stop." He lifted his hand. "I won't act; I shall never 'play' for you again." He was breathless; the witching silence was nothing to what stirred him now. A singular exaltation rose in him, together with the reckless impulse to speak from the mood her vehement confidence had inspired. He gave way to it.

"I know, I know," he said huskily. "I understand all you mean, all you feel, all you wish. It is all echoing here, and here, and here!" He touched his breast, his eyes, and his forehead with the fingers of his long and slender hand. "We sigh and strain our eyes and stretch out our arms in the dark, groping always for the strange blessing that is just beyond our grasp, seeking for the precious unknown that lies just over the horizon! It's what they meant by the pot of gold where the rainbow ends—only, it may be there, after all!"

They stopped unconsciously, and remained standing at the lower end of the Carewe hedge. The western glow had faded, and she was gazing at him through the darkness, leaning forward, never dreaming that her tight grasp had broken the sticks of the little pink fan.

"Yes," she whispered, eagerly. "You are right: you understand!"

He went on, the words coming faster and faster: "We are haunted—you and I—by the wish to know all things, and by the question that lies under every thought we have: the agonizing Whither? Isn't it like that? It is really death that makes us think. You are a good Catholic: you go to mass; but you wish to know. Does God reign, or did it all happen? Sometimes it seems so deadly probable that the universe just was, no God to plan it, nothing but things; that we die as sparrows die, and the brain is all the soul we have, a thing that becomes clogged and stops some day. And is that all?"

She shivered slightly, but her steadfast eyes did not shift from him. He threw back his head, and his face, uplifted to the jewelled sky of the moonless night, was beatific in its peacefulness, as he continued in an altered tone, gentle and low:

"I think all questions are answered there. The stars tell it all. When you look at them you know! They have put them on our flag. There are times when this seems but a poor nation: boastful, corrupt, violent, and preparing, as it is now, to steal another country by fraud and war; yet the stars on the flag always make me happy and confident. Do you see the constellations swinging above us, such unimaginable vastnesses, not roving or crashing through the illimitable at haphazard, but moving in more excellent measure, and to a finer rhythm, than the most delicate clockwork man ever made? The great ocean-lines mark our seas with their paths through the water; the fine brains of the earth are behind the ships that sail from port to port, yet how awry the system goes! When does a ship come to her harbor at an hour determined when she sailed? What is a ship beside the smallest moon of the smallest world? But, there above us, moons, worlds, suns, all the infinite cluster of colossi, move into place to the exactness of a hair at the precise instant. That instant has been planned, you see; it is part of a system—and can a system exist that no mind made? Think of the Mind that made this one! Do you believe so inconceivably majestic an Intelligence as that could be anything but good? Ah, when you wonder, look above you; look above you in the night, I say," he cried, his hand upraised like his transfigured face. "Look above you and you will never fear that a sparrow's fall could go unmarked!"

It was not to the stars that she looked, but to the orator, as long as he held that pose, which lasted until a hard-ridden horse came galloping down the street. As it dashed by, though the rider looked neither to right nor left, Miss Betty unconsciously made a feverish clutch at her companion's sleeve, drawing him closer to the hedge.

"It is my father," she said hurriedly in a low voice. "He must not see you. You must never come here. Perhaps—" She paused, then quickly whispered: "You have been very kind to me. Good-night."

He looked at her keenly, and through the dimness saw that her face was shining with excitement. He did not speak again, but, taking a step backward, smiled faintly, bent his head in humble acquiescence, and made a slight gesture of his hand for her to leave him. She set her eyes upon his once more, then turned swiftly and almost ran along the hedge to the gate; but there she stopped and looked back. He was standing where she had left him, his face again uplifted to the sky.

She waved him an uncertain farewell, and ran into the garden, both palms against her burning cheeks.

Night is the great necromancer, and strange are the fabrics he weaves; he lays queer spells; breathes so eerie an intoxication through the dusk; he can cast such glamours about a voice! He is the very king of fairyland.

Miss Betty began to walk rapidly up and down the garden paths, her head bent and her bands still pressed to her cheeks; now and then an unconscious exclamation burst from her, incoherent, more like a gasp than a word. A long time she paced the vigil with her stirring heart, her skirts sweeping the dew from the leaning flowers. Her lips moved often, but only the confused, vehement" Oh, oh!" came from them, until at last she paused in the middle of the garden, away from the trees, where all was open to the sparkling firmament, and extended her arms over her head.

"O, strange teacher," she said aloud, "I take your beautiful stars! I shall know how to learn from them!"

She gazed steadily upward, enrapt, her eyes resplendent with their own starlight.

"Oh, stars, stars, stars!" she whispered.

In the teeth of all wizardry, Night's spells do pass at sunrise; marvellous poems sink to doggerel, mighty dreams to blown ashes and solids regain weight. Miss Betty, waking at daybreak, saw the motes dancing in the sun at her window, and watched them with a placid, unremembering eye. She began to stare at them in a puzzled way, while a look of wonder slowly spread over her face. Suddenly she sat upright, as though something had startled her. Her fingers clenched tightly.

"Ah, if that was playing!"

CHAPTER VIII

A TALE OF A POLITICAL DIFFERENCE

Mr. Carewe was already at the breakfast-table, but the light of his countenance, hidden behind the Rouen Journal, was not vouchsafed to his daughter when she took her place opposite him, nor did he see fit to return her morning greeting, from which she generously concluded that the burning of the two warehouses had meant a severe loss to him.

"I am so sorry, father," she said gently. (She had not called him "papa" since the morning after her ball.) "I hope it isn't to be a great trouble to you." There was no response, and, after waiting for some time, she spoke again, rather tremulously, yet not timidly: "Father?"

He rose, and upon his brow were marked the blackest lines of anger she had ever seen, so that she leaned back from him, startled; but he threw down the open paper before her on the table, and struck it with his clenched fist.

"Read that!" he said. And he stood over her while she read.

There were some grandiloquent headlines: "Miss Elizabeth Carewe an Angel of Mercy! Charming Belle Saves the Lives of Five Prominent Citizens! Her Presence of Mind Prevents Conflagration from Wiping Out the City!" It may be noted that Will Cummings, editor and proprietor of the Journal, had written these tributes, as well as the whole account of the evening's transactions, and Miss Betty loomed as large in Will's narrative as in his good and lovelorn heart. There was very little concerning the fire in the Journal; it was nearly all about Betty. That is one of the misfortunes which pursue a lady who allows an editor to fall in love with her.

However, there was a scant mention of the arrival of the Volunteers "upon the scene" (though none at all at the cause of their delay) and an eloquent paragraph was devoted to their handsome appearance, Mr. Cummings having been one of those who insisted that the new uniforms should be worn. "Soon," said the Journal, "through the daring of the Chief of the Department, and the Captain of the Hook-and-Ladder Company, one of whom placed and mounted the grappling-ladder, over which he was immediately followed by the other carrying the hose, a stream was sent to play upon the devouring element, a feat of derring-do personally witnessed by a majority of our readers. Mr. Vanrevel and Mr. Gray were joined by Eugene Madrillon, Tappingham Marsh, and the editor of this paper, after which occurred the unfortunate accident to the long ladder, leaving the five named gentlemen in their terrible predicament, face to face with death in its most awful form. At this frightful moment "— and all the rest was about Miss Carewe.

As Will himself admitted, he had "laid himself out on that description." One paragraph was composed of short sentences, each beginning with the word "alone." "Alone she entered the shattered door! Alone she set foot upon the first flight of stairs! Alone she ascended the second! Alone she mounted the third. Alone she lifted her hand to the trap! Alone she opened it!" She was declared to have made her appearance to the unfortunate prisoners on the roof, even as "the palm-laden dove to the despairing Noah," and Will also asserted repeatedly that she was the "Heroine of the Hour."

Miss Betty blushed to see her name so blazoned forth in print; but she lacked one kind of vanity, and failed to find good reason for more than a somewhat troubled laughter, the writer's purpose was so manifestly kind in spite of the bizarre result.

"Oh, I wish Mr. Cummings hadn't!" she exclaimed. "It would have been better not to speak of me at all, of course; but I can't see that there is anything to resent—it is so funny!"

"Funny!" Mr. Carewe repeated the word in a cracked falsetto, with the evident intention of mocking her, and at the same time hideously contorted his face into a grotesque idiocy of expression, pursing his lips so extremely, and setting his brows so awry, that his other features were cartooned out of all familiar likeness, effecting an alteration as shocking to behold, in a man of his severe cast of countenance, as was his falsetto mimicry to hear. She rose in a kind of terror, perceiving that this contortion was produced in burlesque of her own expression, and, as he pressed nearer her, stepped back, overturning her chair. She had little recollection of her father during her childhood; and as long as she could remember, no one had spoken to her angrily, or even roughly.

As she retreated from him, he leaned forward, thrusting the hideous mask closer to her white and horror-stricken face.

"You can't see anything to resent in that!" he gibbered. "It's so funny, is it? Funny! Funny! Funny! I'll show you whether it's funny or not, I'll show you!" His voice rose almost to a shriek. "You hang around fires, do you, on the public streets at night? You're a nice one for me to leave in charge of my house while I'm away, you trollop! What did you mean by going up on that roof? You knew that damned Vanrevel was there! You did, I say, you knew it!"

She ran toward the door with a frightened cry; but he got between it and her, menacing her with his upraised open hands, shaking them over her.

"You're a lovely daughter, aren't you!" he shouted hoarsely. "You knew perfectly well who was on that roof, and you went! Didn't you go? Answer me that! If I'd had arms about me when I got there, I'd have shot that man dead! He was on my property, giving orders, the black hound! And when I ordered him out, he told me if I interfered with his work before it was finished, he'd have me thrown out—me that owned the whole place; and there wasn't a man that would lend me a pistol! 'Rescue!' You'd better rescue him from me, you palm-laden dove, for I'll shoot him, I will! I'll kill that dog; and he knows it. He can bluster in a crowd, but he'll hide now! He's a coward and—"

"He came home with me; he brought me home last night!" Her voice rang out in the room like that of some other person, and she hardly knew that it was herself who spoke.

"You lie!" he screamed, and fell back from her, his face working as though under the dominance of some physical disorder, the flesh of it plastic beyond conception, so that she cried out and covered her face with her arm. "You lie! I saw you at the hedge with Crailey Gray, though you thought I didn't. What do you want to lie like that for? Vanrevel didn't even speak to you. I asked Madrillon. You lie!"

He choked upon the words; a racking cough shook him from head to foot; he staggered back and dropped upon her overturned chair, his arms beating the table in front of him, his head jerking spasmodically backward and forward as he gasped for breath.

"Ring the bell," be panted thickly, with an incoherent gesture. "Nelson knows. Ring!"

Nelson evidently knew. He brought brandy and water from the sideboard with no stinting hand, and within ten minutes Mr. Carewe was in his accustomed seat, competent to finish his breakfast. In solitude, however, he sat, and no one guessed his thoughts.

For Miss Betty had fled to her own room, and had bolted the door. She lay upon the bed, shuddering and shivering with nausea and cold, though the day was warm. Then, like a hot pain in her breast, came a homesickness for St. Mary's, and the flood-tide of tears, as she thought of the quiet convent in the sunshine over to the west, the peace of it, and the goodness of everybody there.

"Sister Cecilia!" Her shoulders shook with the great sob that followed this name, dearest to her in the world, convulsively whispered to the pillow "Dear Sister Cecilia!" She patted the white pillow with her hand, as though it were the cool cheek against which she yearned to lay her own. "Ah, you would know—you would know!" With the thought of the serene face of the good Sister, and of the kind arms that would have gone round her in her trouble, her sobbing grew loud and uncontrollable. But she would not have her father hear it, and buried her face deep in the pillow. After a time, she began to grow quieter, turned, and lay with wet eyes staring unseeingly at the wall, her underlip quivering with the deep intake of each broken sigh.

"Oh, stars, stars, stars!" she whispered.

"Missy?" There came a soft knock upon the door and the clink of silver upon china. " Missy?

"What is it?"

So quick was Miss Betty that, although she answered almost at once, the tears were washed away, and she was passing a cool, wet towel over her eyes at the moment she spoke.

"Jass me. I brung yo' breakfas', honey."

Old Nelson's voice was always low and gentle, with a quaver and hesitancy in the utterance; now it was tender and comforting with the comprehension of one in suffering, the extraordinary tact, which the old of his race nearly all come to possess. "Li'l chicken-wing on piece brown toast, honey."

When she opened the door he came in, bending attentively over his tray, and, without a glance toward his young mistress, made some show of fuss and bustle, as he placed it upon a table near the window and drew up a chair for her so that she could sit with her back to the light.

"Dah now!" he exclaimed softly, removing the white napkin and displaying other dainties besides the chicken wing. "Dass de way! Dat ole Mamie in de kitchen, she got her failin's an' her grievin' sins; but de way she do han'le chicken an' biscuit sutney ain't none on 'em! She plead fo' me to ax you how you like dem biscuit."

He kept his head bent low over the table, setting a fork closer to Betty's hand; arranging the plates, then rearranging them, but never turning his eyes in her direction.

"Dat ole Mamie mighty vain, yessuh!" He suffered a very quiet chuckle to escape him. "She did most sutney 'sist dat I ax you ain't you like dem biscuit. She de ve'y vaines' woman in dis State, dat ole Mamie, yessuh!" And now he cast one quick glance out of the corner of his eye at Miss Betty, before venturing a louder chuckle. "She reckon dem biscuit goin' git her by Sain' Petuh when she 'proach de hevumly gates! Uhuh! I tell her she got git redemption fo' de aigs she done ruin dese many yeahs; 'cause she as useless wid an ommelick as a two-day calf on de slick ice!" Here he laughed loud and long. "You jass go and talk wid dat Mamie, some day, Missy; you'll see how vain dat woman is."

"Has father gone out, Nelson?" asked Betty in a low voice.

"Yes'm; he up town." The old man's tone sank at once to the level of her own; became confidential, as one speaks to another in a room where somebody is ill. "He mekkin' perpetration to go down de rivuh dis aft'noon. He say he done broke de news to you dat he goin' 'way. Dey goin' buil' dem wa'house right up, an' yo' pa he necistate go 'way 'count de contrack. He be gone two week', honey," Nelson finished, without too much the air of imparting cheery tidings, but with just enough.

"I am to stay here alone?"

"Law no, Missy! Dat big Miz Tanberry, dass de bes' frien' we all got, she home ag'in, an' yo' pa goin' invite her visit at de house, whiles he gone, an' to stay a mont' aftuh he git back, too, soze she kin go to all de doin's an' junketin's wid you, and talk wid de young mens dat you don' like whiles you talks wid dem you does like."

"What time will father come home?"

"Home? He be gone two week', honey!"

No; I mean to-day."

"Law! He ain' comin' back. Bid me pack de trunk an' ca'y um down to de boat at noon. Den he bid me say far'-ye-well an' a kine good-bye fo' him, honey. 'Say he think you ain't feelin' too well, soze he won't 'sturb ye, hisself, an' dat he unestly do hope you goin' have splen'id time whiles he trabblin'." (Nelson's imagination covered many deficits in his master's courtesy.) "Say he reckon you an' ole Miz Tanberry goin' git 'long mighty nice wid one'nurr. An' dass what me an' Mamie reckon 'spechually boun' to take place, 'cause dat a mighty gay lady, dat big Miz Tanberry, an' ole frien' 'er owah fambly. She 'uz a frien' er yo' momma's, honey."

Miss Betty had begun by making a pretence to eat, only to please the old man, but the vain woman's cookery had been not unduly extolled, and Nelson laughed with pleasure to see the fluffy hiscuits and the chicken wing not nibbled at but actually eaten. This was a healthy young lady, he thought, one who would do the household credit and justify the extravagant pride which kitchen and stable already had in her. He was an old house-servant, therefore he had seen many young ladies go through unhappy hours, and he admired Miss Betty the more because she was the first who had indulged in strong weeping and did not snuffle at intervals afterward. He understood perfectly everything that had passed between father and daughter that morning.

When her breakfast was finished, she turned slowly to the window, and, while her eyes did not refill, a slight twitching of the upper lids made him believe that she was going over the whole scene again in her mind; whereupon he began to move briskly about the room with a busy air, picking up her napkin, dusting a chair with his hand, exchanging the position of the andirons in the fireplace; and, apparently discovering that the portrait of Georges Meilhac was out of line, he set it awry, then straight again, the while be hummed an old "spiritual" of which only the words "Chain de Lion Down" were allowed to be quite audible. They were repeated often, and at each repetition of them he seemed profoundly, though decorously, amused, in a way which might have led to a conjecture that the refrain bore some distant reference to his master's eccentricity of temper. At first be chuckled softly, but at the final iteration of "Chain de Lion Down" burst into outright laughter.

"Honey, my Law!" he exclaimed, "But yo' pa de 'ceivin'dest man! He mighty proud er you!"

"Proud of me!" She turned to him in astonishment.

Nelson's laughter increased. "Hain't be jass de 'ceivin'dest man! Yessuh, he de sot-uppest man in dis town 'count what you done last night. What he say dis mawn', dat jass his way!"

"Ah, no!" said Miss Betty, sadly.

"Yes'm! He proud er you, but he teahbul mad at dat man. He hain't mad at you, but he gotter cuss somebody! Jass reach out fo' de nighes' he kin lay han's on, an' dis mawn' it happen soze it were you, honey. Uhuh! You oughter hearn him ins' night when he come home. Den it were me. Bless God, I ain't keerin'. He weren't mad at me, no mo'n' he were at you. He jass mad!"

Miss Betty looked at the old fellow keenly. He remained, however, apparently unconscious of her scrutiny, and occupied himself with preparations for removing the tray.

"Nelson, what is the quarrel between my father and Mr. Vanrevel?"

He had lifted the tray, but set it down precipitately, bending upon her a surprised and sobered countenance.

"Missy," he said, gravely, "Dey big trouble 'twix' dem two."

"I know," she returned quietly. "What is it?"

"Wha' fo' you ax me, Missy?"

"Because you're the only one I can ask. I don't know anyone here well enough, except you."

Nelson's lips puckered solemnly. "Mist' Vanrevel vote Whig; but he ag'in Texas."

"Well, what if he is?"

"Yo' pa mighty strong fo' Texas."

"No'm, dat ain't hardly de beginnin'. Mist' lanrevel he a Ab'litionist."

"Well? Won't you tell me?"

"Honey, folks roun' heah mos' on 'em like Mist' Vanrevel so well dey ain't hole it up ag'in' him—but, Missy, ef dey one thing topper God's worl' yo' pa do desp'itly and contestably despise, hate, cuss, an' outrageously 'bominate wuss'n' a yaller August spiduh it are a Ab'litionist! He want stomple 'em eve'y las' one under he boot-heel, 'cep'n dat one Mist' Crailey Gray. Dey's a considabul sprinklin' er dem Ab'litionists 'bout de kentry, honey; dey's mo' dat don' know w'ich dey is; an' dey's mo' still dat don' keer. Soze dat why dey go git up a quo'l twix' yo' pa an' dat man; an' 'range to have 'er on a platfawm, de yeah 'fo' de las' campaign; an', suh, dey call de quo'l a de-bate; an' all de folks come in f'um de kentry, an' all de folks in town come, too. De whole possetucky on 'em sit an' listen.

"Fus' yo' pa talk; den Mist' Vanrevel, bofe on 'em mighty cole an' civilized. Den yo' pa git wo'm up, Missy, like he do, 'case he so useter have his own way; 'tain't his fault, he jass cain't help hollerin' an' cussin' if anybody 'pose him; but Mist' Vanrevel he jass as suvvige, but he stay cole, w'ich make yo' pa all de hotter. He holler mighty strong, Missy, an' some de back ranks 'gun snickerin' at him. Uhuh! He fa'r jump, he did; an' den bimeby Mist' Vanrevel he say dat no man oughter be given de pilverige to sell another, ner to wollop him wid a blacksnake, whether he 'buse dat pilverige er not. 'My honabul 'ponent,' s's he, 'Mist' Carewe, rep'sent in hisseif de 'ristocratic slave-ownin' class er de Souf, do' he live in de Nawf an' 'ploy free labor; yit it sca'sely to be b'lieve dat any er you would willin'ly trus' him wid de powah er life an' death ovah yo' own chillun, w'ich is virchously what de slave-ownah p'sess.'"

"Missy, you jass oughter see yo' pa den! He blue in de face an' dance de quadrille on de boa'ds. He leave his cha'h, git up, an' run 'cross to de odder side de platfawm, an' shake be fis' ovah dat man's head, an' screech out how it all lies dat de slaves evah 'ceive sich a treatments. 'Dat all lies, you pu'juh!' he holler. 'All lies, you misabul thief,' he holler. 'All lies, an' you know it, you low-bawn slandah' an' scoun'le!'

"An' wid dat Mist' Vanrevel, be laff in yo' pa face, an' tuhn to de crowd, he did, an' say: 'You reckon dat if dish yuh man a slave-ownah, an' a slave had anguhed him as I have anguhed him tonight, does any er you b'lieve dat dat slave wouldn' be tied up an' whipped tell de blood run, an' den sole down de rivuh to-morrer?'

"Well, suh, 'co'se mos' on 'em b'lieve same as yo' pa; but dat sutney fotch 'em, an' win de de-bate, 'case dey jass natchully lay back an' roah, dey did, Missy; dey laff an' stomp an' holler tell you could a hearn 'em a mild away. An' honey, yo' pa'd a millyum times druther Mist' Vanrevel'd a kilt him dan tuhn de laff on him. He'd shoot a man, honey, ef he jass s'picion him to grin out de cornder his eye at him; an' to stan' up dah wid de whole county fa'r roahin' at him—it's de God's mussy be did'n have no ahms wid him, dat night! Ole Mist' Chen'eth done brung him home, an' yo' pa reach out an' kick me squah' out'n' de liberry winder soon's he ketch sight er me!" The old man's gravity gave way to his enjoyment of the recollection, and he threw back his head to laugh. "He sho' did, honey! Uhuh! Ho, ho, ho! He sho' did, honey, he sho' did!"

Nevertheless, as he lifted the tray again and crossed the room to go, his solemnity returned. "Missy," he said earnestly," ef dat young gelmun fall in love wid you, w'ich I knows he will ef he ketch sight er you, lemme say dis, an' please fo' to ba'h in mine: better have nuttin' do wid him fo' he own sake; an' 'bove all, keep him fur sway fum dese p'emises. Don' let him come in a mild er dis house."

"Nelson, was that all the quarrel between them?"

"Blessed Mussy! ain' dat 'nough? Ef dey's any mo' I ain' hearn what dat part were," he answered quickly, but with a dogged tightening of the lips which convinced Miss Betty that he knew very well.

"Nelson, what was the rest of it?"

"Please, Missy, I got pack yo' pa trunk; an' it time, long ago, fer me to be at my wu'k." He was half out of the door.

"What was the rest of it? " she repeated quietly.

"Now, honey," he returned with a deprecatory shake of his head, "I got my own wu'k 'tend to; an' I ain't nevah ax nobody what 'twas, an' I ain't goin' ax 'em. An' lemme jass beg you f oiler de ole man's advice: you do de same, 'case nobody ain't goin' tell you. All I know is dat it come later and were somep'n 'bout dat riprarin Crailey Gray. Yo' pa he sent a channelge to Mist' Vanrevel, an' Mist' Vanrevel 'fuse to fight him 'cause he say he don' b'lieve shootin' yo' pa goin' do yo' pa any good, an' he still got hope mekkin' good citizen outer him. Dat brung de laff on yo' pa ag'in; an' he 'clare to God ef he ketch Vanrevel on any groun' er hisn he shoot him like a mad dog. 'Pon my livin' soul he mean dem wuds, Missy! Dey had hard 'nough time las' night keepin' him fum teahin' dat man to pieces at de fiah. You mus' keep dat young gelmun 'way fum heah!"

"He came home with me last night, Nelson; I told father so."

"Yes'm. Yo' pa tole me you say dat, but he reckon you done it to mek him madder, 'cause you mad, too. He say he done see dat Crailey Gray comin' 'long de hedge wid you."

"He was mistaken, it was Mr. Vanrevel."

Nelson rolled his eyes fervently to heaven. "Den dat young man run pintedly on he death! Ef you want keep us all dis side er de Jawdan Rivuh, don' let him set foot in dis neighbo'hood when yo' pa come back! An', honey—" his voice sank to a penetrating whisper—" 'fo' I do a lick er wu'k I goin' out in de stable an' git down on my knees an' retu'n thanksgiving to de good God 'case he hole Carewe Street in de dahkness las' night!"

This was the speech he chose for his exit, but, after closing the door behind him, he opened it again, and said, cheerfully:

"Soon's I git de trunk fix f' yo' pa, I bring 'roun' dat bay colt wid de side saddle. You better set 'bout gittin' on yo' ridin'-habit, Missy. De roads is mighty good dis sunshiny wedduh."

" Nelson? "

"Do you think such an attack as father had this morning—is—dangerous?"

He had hoped for another chance to laugh violently before he left her, and this completely fitted his desire. "Ho, ho, he!" he shouted. "No'm, no, no, honey! He jass git so mad it mek him sick. You couldn' kill dat man wid a broad-ax, Missy!"

And he went down the hail leaving the reverberations of his hilarity behind him. The purpose of his visit had been effected, for, when Miss Betty appeared upon the horse-block in her green habit and gauntlets, she was smiling; so that only a woman—or a wise old man—could have guessed that she had wept bitterly that morning.

She cantered out to the flat, open country to the east, where she found soft dirt-roads that were good for the bay colt's feet, and she reached a cross-road several miles from town before she was overcome by the conviction that she was a wicked and ungrateful girl. She could not place the exact spot of her guilt, but she knew it was there, somewhere, since she felt herself a guilty thing.

For the picture which Nelson had drawn rose before her: the one man standing alone in his rage on the platform, overwhelmed by his calm young adversary, beaten and made the butt of laughter for a thousand. Her father had been in the wrong in that quarrel, and somehow she was sure, too, he must have been wrong in the "personal" one, as well: the mysterious difficulty over Fanchon's Mr. Gray, who had looked so ashamed last night. What feud could they make over him, of all people in the world? He looked strong enough to take care of his own quarrels, even if he was so rigorously bound by Fanchon's apron-string when it came to a word with another girl!

But the conclusion that her father had been in error did not lessen the pathetic appeal of the solitary figure facing the ridicule of the crowd. She felt that he always honestly believed himself in the right; she knew that he was vain; that he had an almost monstrous conception of his dignity; and, realizing the bitterness of that public humiliation which he had undergone, she understood the wrath, the unspeakable pain and sense of outrage, which must have possessed him.

And now she was letting him go forth upon a journey—his way beset with the chances of illness and accident—whence he might never return; she was letting him go without seeing him again; letting him go with no word of farewell from his daughter. In brief: she was a wicked girl. She turned the colt's head abruptly to the west and touched his flanks with her whip.

So it fell out that as the packet foamed its passage backward from Carewe's wharf into the current, the owner of the boat, standing upon the hurricane deck, heard a cry from the shore, and turned to behold his daughter dash down to the very end of the wharf on the well-lathered colt. Miss Betty's hair was blown about her face; her cheeks were rosy, her eager eyes sparkling from more than the hard riding.

"Papa!" she cried, "I'm sorry!"

She leaned forward out of the saddle, extending her arms to him appealingly in a charming gesture, and, absolutely ignoring the idlers on the wharf and the passengers on the steamer, was singly intent upon the tall figure on the hurricane-deck. "Papa—good-by. Please forgive me!"

"By the Almighty, but that's a fine woman!" said the captain of the boat to a passenger from Rouen. "Is she his daughter?"

"Please forgive me!" the clear voice came again, with its quaver of entreaty, across the widening water; and then, as Mr. Carewe made no sign, by word or movement, of hearing her, and stood without the slightest alteration of his attitude, she cried to him once more:

"Good-by!"

The paddle-wheels reversed; the boat swung down the river, Mr. Carewe still standing immovable on the hurricane-deck, while, to the gaze of those on the steamer, the figure on the bay colt at the end of the wharf began to grow smaller and smaller. She was waving her handkerchief in farewell, and they could see the little white speck in the distance, dimmer and dimmer, yet fluttering still as they passed out of sight round the bend nearly three-quarters of a mile below.

CHAPTER IX

THE RULE OF THE REGENT

Betty never forgot her first sight of the old friend of her family. Returning with a sad heart, she was walking the colt slowly through the carriage-gates, when an extravagantly stout lady, in green muslin illustrated with huge red flowers, came out upon the porch and waved a fat arm to the girl. The visitor wore a dark-green turban and a Cashmere shawl, while the expanse of her skirts was nothing short of magnificent: some cathedral-dome seemed to have been misplaced and the lady dropped into it. Her outstretched hand terrified Betty: how was she to approach near enough to take it?

Mrs. Tanberry was about sixty, looked forty, and at first you might have guessed she weighed nearly three hundred, but the lightness of her smile and the actual buoyancy which she somehow imparted to her whole dominion lessened that by at least a hundred-weight. She ballooned out to the horse-block with a billowy rush somewhere between bounding and soaring; and Miss Betty slid down from the colt, who shied violently, to find herself enveloped, in spite of the dome, in a vast surf of green and red muslin.

"My charming girl!" exclaimed the lady vehemently, in a

voice of such husky richness, of such merriment and unction of delight, that it fell upon Miss Betty's ear with more of the quality of sheer gayety than any she had ever heard. "Beautiful child! What a beautiful child you are!"

She kissed the girl resoundingly on both cheeks; stepped back from her and laughed, and clapped her fat hands, which were covered with flashing rings. "Oh, but you are a true blue Beauty! You're a Princess! I am Mrs. Tanberry, Jane Tanberry, young Janie Tanberry. I haven't seen you since you were a baby and your pretty mother was a girl like us!"

"You are so kind to come," said Betty hesitatingly. "I shall try to be very obedient."

"Obedient!" Mrs. Tanberry uttered the word with a shriek. "You'll be nothing of the kind. I am the light-mindedest woman in the universe, and anyone who obeyed me would be embroiled in everlasting trouble every second in the day. You'll find that I am the one that needs looking after, my charmer!"

She tapped Miss Betty's cheek with her jeweled fingers as the two mounted the veranda steps. "It will be worry enough for you to obey yourself; a body sees that at the first blush. You have conscience in your forehead and rebellion in your chin. Ha, ha, ha!" Here Mrs. Tanberry sat upon, and obliterated, a large chair, Miss Carewe taking a stool at her knee.

"People of our age oughtn't to be bothered with obeying; there'll be time enough for that when we get old and can't enjoy anything. Ha, ha!"

Mrs. Tanberry punctuated her observations with short volleys of husky laughter, so abrupt in both discharge and cessation that, until Miss Betty became accustomed to the habit, she was apt to start slightly at each salvo. "I had a husband—once," the lady resumed, "but only once, my friend! He had ideas like your father's—your father is such an imbecile!—and he thought that wives, sisters, daughters, and such like ought to be obedient: that is, the rest of the world was wrong unless it was right; and right was just his own little, teeny-squeeny prejudices and emotions dressed up for a crazy masquerade as Facts. Poor man! He only lasted about a year!" And Mrs. Tanberry laughed heartily.

"They've been at me time and again to take another." She lowered her voice and leaned toward Betty confidentially. "Not I! I'd be willing to engage myself to Crailey Gray (though Crailey hasn't got round to me yet) for I don't mind just being engaged, my dear; but they'll have to invent something better than a man before I marry any one of 'em again! But I love 'em, I do, the Charming Billies! And you'll see how they follow me!" She patted the girl's shoulder, her small eyes beaming quizzically. "We'll have the gayest house in Rouen, ladybird! The young men all go to the Bareauds', but they'll come here now, and we'll have the Bareauds along with 'em. I've been away a long time, just finished unpacking yesterday night when your father came in after the fire— Whoo! what a state he was in with that devilish temper of his! Didn't I snap him up when he asked me to come and stay with you? Ha, ha! I'd have come, even if you hadn't been beautiful; but I was wild to be your playmate, for I'd heard nothing but 'Miss Betty Carewe, Miss Betty Carewe' from everybody I saw, since the minute my stage came in. You set 'em all mad at your ball, and I knew we'd make a glorious house-full, you and I! Some of the vagabonds will turn up this very evening, you'll see if they don't. Ha, ha! The way they follow me!"

Mrs. Tanberry was irresistible: she filled the whole place

otherwise than by the mere material voluminousness of her; bubbling over with froth of nonsense which flew through the house, driven by her energy, like sea-foam on a spring gale; and the day, so discordantly begun for Miss Betty, grew musical with her own laughter, answering the husky staccato of the vivacious newcomer. Nelson waited upon them at table, radiant, his smile like the keyboard of an ebony piano, and his disappearances into the kitchen were accomplished by means of a surreptitious double-shuffle, and followed by the cachinnating echoes of the vain Mamie's reception of the visitor's sallies, which Nelson hastily retailed in passing.

Nor was Mrs. Tanberry's prediction allowed to go unfulfilled regarding the advent of those persons whom she had designated as vagabonds. It may have been out of deference to Mr. Carewe's sense of decorum (or from a cautious regard of what he was liable to do when he considered that sense outraged) that the gallants of Rouen had placed themselves under the severe restraint of allowing three days to elapse after their introduction to Miss Carewe before they "paid their respects at the house ;" but, be that as it may, the dictator was now safely under way down the Rouen River, and Mrs. Tanberry reigned in his stead. Thus, at about eight o'clock that evening, the two ladies sat in the library engaged in conversation—though, for the sake of accuracy, it should be said that Mrs. Tanberry was engaged in conversation, Miss Betty in giving ear—when their attention was arrested by sounds of a somewhat musical nature from the lawn, which sounds were immediately identified as emanating from a flute and violin.

Mrs. Tanberry bounded across the room like a public building caught by a cyclone, and, dashing at the candles, "Blow 'em out, blow 'em out!" she exclaimed, suiting the action to the word in a fluster of excitement.

"Why?" asked Miss Carewe, startled, as she rose to her feet. The candles were out before the question.

"'Why!" repeated the merry, husky voice in the darkness. "My goodness, child precious, those vagabonds are here! To think of your never having been serenaded before!"

She drew the girl to the window and pointed to a group of dim figures near the iliac bushes. "The dear, delightful vagabonds!" she chuckled. "I knew they'd come! It's the beautiful Tappingham Marsh with his fiddle, and young Jeff Bareaud with his flute, and 'Gene Madrillon and little Frank Chenowith and thin Will Cummings to sing. Hark to the rascals!"

It is perfectly truthful to say that the violin and flute executed the prelude, and then the trio sounded full on the evening air, the more effective chords obligingly drawn out as long as the breath in the singers could hold them, in order to allow the two fair auditors complete benefit of the harmony. They sang "The Harp that Once Thro' Tara's Halls," and followed it with "Long, Long Ago."

"That," Mrs. Tanberry whispered, between stifled gusts of almost uncontrollable laughter, "is meant for just me!"

"Tell me the tales that to me were so dear," entreated the trio.

"I told 'em plenty!" gurgled the enlivening widow. "And I expect between us we can get up some more." "Now you are come my grief is removed," they sang.

"They mean your father is on his way to St. Louis," remarked Mrs. Tanberry.

"Let me forget that so long you have roved, Let me believe

that you love as you loved, Long, long ago, long ago."

"Applaud, applaud!" whispered Mrs. Tanberry, encouraging the minstrels by a hearty clapping of hands.

Hereupon dissension arose among the quintet, evidently a dispute in regard to their next selection; one of the gentlemen appearing more than merely to suggest a solo by himself, while the others too frankly expressed adverse opinions upon the value of the offering. The argument became heated, and in spite of many a "Sh!" and "Not so loud!" the ill-suppressed voice of the intending soloist, Mr. Chenoweth, could be heard vehemently to exclaim: "I will! I learned it especially for this occasion. I will sing it!"

His determination, patently, was not to be balked without physical encounter, consequently he was permitted to advance some paces from the lilac bushes, where he delivered himself, in an earnest and plaintive tenor, of the following morbid instructions, to which the violin played an obligato in tremulo, so execrable, and so excruciatingly discordant, that Mr. Chenoweth's subsequent charge that it was done with a deliberately evil intention could never be successfully opposed:

"Go! Forget me! Why should Sorrow O'er that brow a shadow fling? Go! Forget me, and, to-morrow, Brightly smile and sweetly sing!"

Smile! tho' I may not be near thee; Smile! tho' I may never see thee; May thy soul with pleasure shine Lasting as this gloom of mine!"

Miss Carewe complied at once with the request; while her companion, unable to stop with the slight expression of pleasure demanded by the songster, threw herself upon a sofa and gave way to the mirth that consumed her.

Then the candles were relit, the serenaders invited within; Nelson came bearing cake and wine, and the house was made merry. Presently, the romp, Virginia Bareaud, making her appearance on the arm of General Trumble, Mrs. Tanberry led them all in a hearty game of Blind-man's Buff, followed by as hearty a dancing of Dan Tucker. After that, a quadrille being proposed, Mrs. Tanberry suggested that Jefferson should run home and bring Fanchon for the fourth lady. However, Virginia explained that she had endeavored to persuade both her sister and Mr. Gray to accompany the General and herself, but that Mr. Gray had complained of indisposition, having suffered greatly from headache, on account of inhaling so much smoke at the warehouse fire; and, of course, Fanchon would not leave him. (Miss Carewe permitted herself the slightest shrug of the shoulders.)

So they danced the quadrille with Jefferson at the piano and Mr. Marsh performing in the character of a lady, a proceeding most unacceptable to the General, whom Mrs. Tanberry forced to be his partner. And thus the evening passed gayly away, and but too quickly, to join the ghosts of all the other evenings since time began; and each of the little company had added a cheerful sprite to the long rows of those varied shades that the after years bring to revisit us, so many with pathetic reproach, so many bearing a tragic burden of faces that we cannot make even to weep again, and so few with simple merriment and lightheartedness. Tappingham Marsh spoke the truth, indeed, when he exclaimed in parting, "O rare Mrs. Tanberry!"

But the house had not done with serenades that night. The guests had long since departed; the windows were still and dark under the wan old moon, which had risen lamely, looking unfamiliar and not half itself; the air bore an odor of lateness, and nothing moved; when a delicate harmony stole out of the shadows beyond the misty garden. Low but resonant chords sounded on the heavier strings of a guitar, while above them, upon the lighter wires, rippled a slender, tinkling melody that wooed the slumberer to a delicious half-wakefulness, as dreamily, as tenderly, as the croon of rain on the roof soothes a child to sleep. Under the artist's cunning touch the instrument was both the accompaniment and the song; and Miss Betty, at first taking the music to be a wandering thread in the fabric of her own bright dreams, drifted gradually to consciousness to find herself smiling. Her eyes opened wide, but half closed again with the ineffable sweetness of the sound.

Then a voice was heard, eerily low, yet gallant and clear, a vibrant baritone, singing to the guitar.

"My lady's hair, That dark delight, Is both as fair And dusk as night. I know some lovelorn hearts that beat In time to moonbeam twinklings fleet, That dance and glance like jewels there, Emblazoning the raven hair!

"Ah, raven hair! So dark and bright, What loves lie there Enmeshed, to-night? I know some sighing lads that say Their hearts were snared and torn away; And now as pearls one fate they share, Entangled in the raven hair.

"Ah, raven hair, >From such a plight Could you not spare One acolyte? I know a broken heart that went To serve you but as ornament. Alas! a ruby now you wear, Ensanguining the raven hair!"

The song had grown fainter and fainter, the singer moving away as he sang, and the last lines were almost inaudible in the distance The guitar could be heard for a moment or two more, then silence came again. It was broken by a rustling in the room next to Miss Betty's, and Mrs. Tanberry called softly through the open door:

"Princess, are you awake? Did you hear that serenade? "

After a pause the answer came hesitatingly in a small, faltering voice: "Yes—if it was one. I thought perhaps he was only singing as he passed along the street."

"Aha!" ejaculated Mrs. Tanberry, abruptly, as though she had made an unexpected discovery. "You knew better; and this was a serenade that you did not laugh at. Beautiful, I wouldn't let it go any farther, even while your father is gone. Something might occur that would bring him home without warning—such things have happened. Tom Vanrevel ought to be kept far away from this house."

"Oh, it was not he," returned Miss Betty, quickly. "It was Mr. Gray. Didn't you—"

"My dear," interrupted the other, "Crailey Gray's specialty is talking. Most of the vagabonds can sing and play a bit, and so can Crailey, particularly when he's had a few bowls of punch; but when Tom Vanrevel touches the guitar and lifts up his voice to sing, there isn't an angel in heaven that wouldn't quit the place and come to hear him! Crailey wrote those words to Virginia Bareaud. (Her hair is even darker than yours, you know.) That was when he was being engaged to her; and Tom must have set the music to 'em lately, and now comes here to sing 'em to you; and well enough they fit you! But you must keep him away, Princess."

Nevertheless, Betty knew the voice was not that which had bid her look to the stars, and she remained convinced that it belonged to Mr. Crailey Gray, who had been too ill, a few hours earlier, to leave the Bareaud house, and now, with

Fanchon's kisses on his lips, came stealing into her garden and sang to her a song he had made for another girl!

And the angels would leave heaven to listen when he sang, would they? Poor Fanchon! No wonder she held him so tightly in leading strings! He might risk his life all he wished at the end of a grappling-ladder, dangling in a fiery cloud above nothing; but when it came to—ah, well, poor Fanchon! Did she invent the headaches for him, or did she make him invent them for himself?

If there was one person in the world whom Miss Betty held in bitter contempt and scorn, it was the owner of that voice and that guitar.

CHAPTER X

ECHOES OF A SERENADE

More than three gentlemen of Rouen wore their hearts in their eyes for any fool to gaze upon; but three was the number of those who told their love before the end of the first week of Mr. Carewe's absence, and told it in spite of Mrs. Tanberry's utmost effort to preserve, at all times, a conjunction between herself and Miss Betty. For the good lady, foreseeing these declarations much more surely than did the subject of them, wished to spare her lovely charge the pain of listening to them.

Miss Carewe honored each of the lorn three with few minutes of gravity; but the gentle refusal prevented never a swain from being as truly her follower as before; not that she resorted to the poor device of half-dismissal, the every-day method of the school-girl flirt, who thus keeps the lads in dalliance, but because, even for the rejected, it was a delight to be near her. For that matter, it is said that no one ever had enough of the mere looking at her. Also, her talk was enlivening even to the lively, being spiced with surprising turns and amiably seasoned with the art of badinage. To use the phrase of the time, she possessed the accomplishments, an antiquated charm now on the point of disappearing, so carefully has it been snubbed under whenever exhibited. The pursuing wraith of the young, it comes to sit, a ghost at every banquet, driving the flower of our youth to unheard-of exertions in search of escape, to dubious diplomacy, to dismal inaction, or to wine; yet time was when they set their hearts on "the accomplishments."

Miss Betty Carewe at her harp, ah! it was a dainty picture: the clear profile, with the dark hair low across the temple, silhouetted duskily, in the cool, shadowy room, against the open window; the slender figure, one arm curving between you and the strings, the other gleaming behind them; the delicate little sandal stealing from the white froth of silk and lace to caress the pedal; the nimble hands fluttering across the long strands, "Like white blossoms borne on slanting lines of rain ;" and the great gold harp rising to catch a javelin of sunshine that pierced the vines at the window where the honeysuckles swung their skirts to the refrain—it was a picture to return many a long year afterward, and thrill the reveries of old men who were then young. And, following the light cascading ripples of the harp, when her low contralto lifted in one of the "old songs," she often turned inquiringly to see if the listener liked the music, and her brilliant, dark eyes would rest on his with an appeal that blinded his entranced soul. She meant it for the mere indication of a friendly wish to suit his tastes, but it looked like the divine humility of love. Nobody wondered that General Trumble should fall to verse-making in his old age.

She sketched magnificently. This is the very strongest support for the assertion: Frank Chenoweth and Tappingham Marsh agreed, with tears of enthusiasm, that "magnificently" was the only word. They came to this conclusion as they sat together at the end of a long dinner (at which very little had been eaten) after a day's picnic by the river. Miss Carewe had been of their company, and Tappingham and Chenoweth found each his opportunity in the afternoon. The party was small, and no one had been able to effect a total uncon-sciousness of the maneuvers of the two gentlemen. Even Fanchon Bareaud comprehended languidly, though she was more blurred than ever, and her far-away eyes belied the mechanical vivacity of her manner, for Crailey was thirty miles down the river, with a fishing-rod neatly packed in a leather case.

Mr. Vanrevel, of course, was not invited; no one would have thought of asking him to join a small party of which Robert Carewe's daughter was to be a member. But it was happiness enough for Tom, that night, to lie hidden in the shrubbery, looking up at the stars between the leaves, while he listened to her harp, and borne through the open window on enchanted airs, the voice of Elizabeth Carewe singing "Robin Adair."

It was now that the town indulged its liveliest spirit; never an evening lacked its junketing, while the happy folk of Rouen set the early summer to music. Serenade, dance, and song for them, the light-hearts, young and old making gay together! It was all laughter, either in sunshine or by candlelight, undisturbed by the far thunder below the southern horizon, where Zachary Taylor had pitched his tent, upon the Rio Grande.

One fair evening, soon after that excursion which had proved fatal to the hopes of the handsome Tappingham and of the youthful Chenoweth, it was the privilege of Mr. Thomas Vanrevel to assist Miss Carewe and her chaperon from their carriage, as they drove up to a dance at the Bareauds'. This good fortune fell only to great deserving, for he had spent an hour lurking outside the house in the hope of performing such offices for them.

Heaven was in his soul and the breath departed out of his

body, when, after a moment of hesitation, Miss Betty's little lace-gauntleted glove was placed in his hand, and her white slipper shimmered out from the lilac flounces of her dress to fall like a benediction, he thought, on each of the carriage-steps.

It was the age of garlands; they wreathed the Muses, the Seasons, and their speech, so the women wore wreaths in their hair, and Miss Betty's that night was of marguerites. "Read your fortune in them all," whispered Tom's heart, "and of whomsoever you wish to learn, every petal will say 'He loves you; none declare, He loves you not!'"

She bowed slightly, but did not speak to him, which was perhaps a better reception than that accorded the young man by her companion. "Oh, it's you, is it!" was Mrs. Tanberry's courteous observation as she canted the vehicle in her descent. She looked sharply at Miss Betty, and even the small glow of the carriage-lamps showed that the girl's cheeks had flushed very red. Mr. Vanrevel, on the contrary, was pale.

They stood for a moment in awkward silence, while, from the lighted house where the flying figures circled, came the waltz: " I dreamt that I dwe-helt in ma-har-ble halls." Tom's own dreams were much wilder than the gypsy girl's; he knew that; yet he spoke out bravely:

"Will you dance the two first with me?"

Miss Betty bit her lip, frowned, turned away, and, vouchsafing no reply, walked toward the house with her eyes fixed on the ground; but just as they reached the door she flashed over him a look that scorched him from head to foot, and sent his spirits down through the soles of his boots to excavate a grotto in the depths of the earth, so charged it was with wrathful pity and contempt.

"Yes!" she said abruptly, and followed Mrs. Tanberry to the dressing-room.

The elder lady shook her head solemnly as she emerged from the enormous folds of a yellow silk cloak. "Ah, Princess," she said, touching the girl's shoulder with her jeweled hand, "I told you I was a very foolish woman, and I am, but not so foolish as to offer advice often. Yet, believe me, it won't do. I think that is one of the greatest young men I ever knew, and it's a pity—but it won't do."

Miss Betty kept her face away from her guardian for a moment. No inconsiderable amount of information had drifted to her, from here and there, regarding the career of Crailey Gray, and she thought how intensely she would have hated any person in the world except Mrs. Tanberry for presuming to think she needed to be warned against the charms of this serenading lady-killer, who was the property of another girl.

"You must keep him away, I think," ventured Mrs. Tanberry, gently.

At that Betty turned to her and said, sharply:

"I will. After this, please let us never speak of him again."

A slow nod of the other's turbaned head indicated the gravest acquiescence. She saw that her companion's cheeks were still crimson. "I understand," said she.

A buzz of whispering, like a July beetle, followed Miss Carewe and her partner about the room during the next dance. How had Tom managed it? Had her father never told her? Who had dared to introduce them? Fanchon was the only one who knew, and as she whirled by with Will Cummings, she raised her absent glance long enough to give Tom an affectionate and warning shake of the head.

Tom did not see this; Miss Carewe did. Alas! She smiled upon him instantly and looked deep into his eyes. It was the third time.

She was not afraid of this man-flirt; he was to be settled with once and forever. She intended to avenge both Fanchon and herself; yet it is a hazardous game, this piercing of eye with eye, because the point which seeks to penetrate may soften and melt, leaving one defenseless. For perhaps ten seconds that straight look lasted, while it seemed to her that she read clear into the soul of him, and to behold it, through some befooling magic, as strong, tender, wise, and true, as his outward appearance would have made an innocent stranger believe him; for he looked all these things; she admitted that much; and he had an air of distinction and resource beyond any she had ever known, even in the wild scramble for her kitten he had not lost it. So, for ten seconds, which may be a long time, she saw a man such as she had dreamed, and she did not believe her sight, because she had no desire to be as credulous as the others, to be as easily cheated as that poor Fanchon!

The luckless Tom found his own feet beautiful on the mountains, and, treading the heights with airy steps, appeared to himself wonderful and glorified—he was waltzing with Miss Betty He breathed the entrancing words to himself, over and over: it was true, he was waltzing with Miss Betty Carewe! Her glove lay warm and light within his own; his fingers clasped that ineffable lilac and white brocade waist. Sometimes her hair came within an inch of his cheek, and then he rose outright from the hilltops and floated in a golden mist.

The glamour of which the Incroyable had planned to tell her some day, surrounded Tom, and it seemed to him that the whole world was covered with a beautiful light like a carpet, which was but the radiance of this adorable girl whom his gloves and coat-sleeve were permitted to touch. When the music stopped, they followed in the train of other couples seeking the coolness of out-of-doors for the interval, and Tom, in his soul, laughed at all other men with illimitable condescension.

"Stop here," she said, as they reached the open gate. He was walking out of it, his head in the air, and Miss Betty on his arm. Apparently, he would have walked straight across the State. It was the happiest moment he had ever known.

He wanted to say something wonderful to her; his speech should be like the music and glory and lire that was in him; therefore he was shocked to hear himself remarking, with an inanity of utterance that sickened him:

"Oh, here's the gate, isn't it?"

Her answer was a short laugh. "You mean you wish to persuade me that you had forgotten it was there?"

"I did not see it," he protested, lamentably.

"No?"

"I wasn't thinking of it."

"Indeed! You were 'lost in thoughts of '—"

"Of you!" he said, before he could check himself.

"Yes?" Her tone was as quietly contemptuous as she could

make it. "How very frank of you! May I ask: Are you convinced that speeches of that sort are always to a lady's liking?"

"No," he answered humbly, and hung his head. Then she threw the question at him abruptly:

"Was it you who came to sing in our garden?"

There was a long pause before a profound sigh came tremulously from the darkness, like a sad and tender confession. "Yes."

"I thought so!" she exclaimed. "Mrs. Tanberry thought it was someone else; but I knew that it was you."

"Yes, you are right," he said, quietly. "It was I. It was my only way to tell you what you know now."

"Of course!" She set it all aside with those two words and the slightest gesture of her hand. " It was a song made for another girl, I believe?" she asked lightly, and with an icy smile, inquired farther: "For the one—the one before the last, I understand?"

He lifted his head, surprised. "What has that to do with it? The music was made for you—but then, I think all music was made for you."

"Leave the music out of it, if you please," she said, impatiently. "Your talents make you modest! No doubt you consider it unmaidenly in me to have referred to the serenade before you spoke of it; but I am not one to cast down my eyes and let it pass. No, nor one too sweet to face the truth, either!" she cried with sudden passion. "To sing that song in the way you did, meant-oh, you thought I would flirt with you! What right had you to come with such a song to me?

Tom intended only to disclaim the presumption, so far from his thoughts, that his song had moved her, for he could see that her attack was prompted by her inexplicable impression that he had assumed the attitude of a conqueror, but his explanation began unfortunately.

"Forgive me. I think you have completely misunderstood; you thought it meant something I did not intend, at all, and—"

"What!" she said, and her eyes blazed, for now she beheld him as the arrant sneak of the world. He, the lady-killer, with his hypocritical air of strength and melancholy sweetness, the leader of drunken revels, and, by reputation, the town Lothario and Light-o'-Love, under promise of marriage to Fanchon Bareaud, had tried to make love to another girl, and now his cowardice in trying to disclaim what he had done lent him the insolence to say to this other: "My child, you are betrayed by your youth and conceit; you exaggerate my meaning. I had no intention to distinguish you by coquetting with you!" This was her interpretation of him; and her indignation was not lessened by the inevitable conclusion that he, who had been through so many scenes with women, secretly found her simplicity diverting. Miss Betty had a little of her father in her; while it was part of her youth, too, that, of all things she could least endure the shadow of a smile at her own expense.

"Oh, oh!" she cried, her voice shaking with anger. "I suppose your bad heart is half-choked with your laughter at me."

She turned from him swiftly, and left him.

Almost running, she entered the house, and hurried to a seat by Mrs. Tanberry, nestling to her like a young sapling on a hillside. Instantaneously, several gentlemen, who had hastily acquitted themselves of various obligations in order to seek her, sprang forward with eager greetings, so that when the stricken Tom, dazed and confounded by his evil luck, followed her at about five paces, he found himself confronted by an impenetrable abbatis formed by the spiked tails of the coats of General Trumble, Madrillon, Tappingham Marsh, Cummings and Jefferson Bareaud. Within this fortification rang out laughter and sally from Miss Carewe; her color was high and her eyes sparkled never more brightly.

Flourish and alarums sounded for a quadrille. Each of the semi-circle, firmly elbowing his neighbor, begged the dance of Miss Betty; but Tom was himself again, and laid a long, strong hand on Madrillon's shoulder, pressed him gently aside, and said:

"Forgive me; Miss Carewe has honored me by the promise of this quadrille."

He bowed, offering his arm, and none of them was too vain to envy that bow and gesture.

For a moment he remained waiting. Miss Carewe rose slowly, and, directly facing him, said in composed and even voice: "You force me to beg you never to address me again."

She placed her hand on the General's arm, turning her back squarely upon Tom.

In addition to those who heard, many persons in that part of the room saw the affront and paused in arrested attitudes; others, observing these, turned inquiringly, so that sudden silence fell, broken only by the voice of Miss Betty as she moved away, talking cheerily to the General. Tom was left standing alone in the broken semicircle.

All the eyes swept from her to him and back; then everyone began to talk hastily about nothing. The young man's humiliation was public.

He went to the door under cover of the movement of the various couples to find places in the quadrille, yet every sidelong glance in the room still rested upon him, and he knew it. He remained in the ball, alone, through that dance, and at its conclusion, walked slowly through the rooms, speaking to people, here and there, as though nothing had happened, but when the music sounded again, he went to the dressing-room, found his hat and cloak, and left the house. For a while he stood on the opposite side of the street, watching the lighted windows, and twice he caught sight of the lilac and white brocade, the dark hair, and the wreath of marguerites. Then, with a hot pain in his breast, and the step of a Grenadier, he marched down the street.

In the carriage Mrs. Tanberry took Betty's hand in hers. "I'll do as you wish, child," she said, "and never speak to you of him again as long as I live, except this once. I think it was best for his own sake as well as yours, but—"

"He needed a lesson," interrupted Miss Betty, wearily. She had danced long and hard, and she was very tired.

Mrs. Tanberry's staccato laugh came out irrepressibly. "All the vagabonds do, Princess!" she cried. "And I think they are getting it."

"No, no, I don't mean—"

"We've turned their heads, my dear, between us, you and I; and we'll have to turn 'em again, or they'll break their necks looking over their shoulders at us, the owls!" She pressed the girl's hand affectionately. "But you'll let me say something just once, and forgive me because we're the same foolish age, you know. It's only this: The next young man you suppress, take him off in a corner! Lead him away from the crowd where he won't have to stand and let them look at him afterward. That's all, my dear, and you mustn't mind."

"I'm not sorry!" said Miss Betty hotly. "I'm not sorry!"

"No, no," said Mrs. Tanberry, soothingly. "It was better this time to do just what you did. I'd have done it myself, to make quite sure he would keep away—because I like him."

"I'm not sorry!" said Miss Betty again.

"I'm not sorry!" she repeated and reiterated to herself after Mrs. Tanberry had gone to bed. She had sunk into a chair in the library with a book, and "I'm not sorry!" she whispered as the open unread page blurred before her, "I'm not sorry!" He had needed his lesson; but she had to bear the recollection of how white his face went when he received it. Her affront had put about him a strange loneliness: the one figure with the stilled crowd staring; it had made a picture from which her mind's eye had been unable to escape, danced she never so hard and late. Unconsciously, Robert Carewe's daughter had avenged the other figure which had stood in lonely humiliation before the staring eyes.

"I'm not sorry!" Ah, did they think it was in her to hurt any living thing in the world? The book dropped from her lap, and she bowed her head upon her hands. "I'm not sorry! "— and tears upon the small lace gauntlets!

She saw them, and with an incoherent exclamation, half self-pitying, half impatient, ran out to the stars above her garden.

She was there for perhaps half an hour, and just before she

returned to the house she did a singular thing.

Standing where all was clear to the sky, where she had stood after her talk with the Incroyable, when he had bid her look to the stars, she raised her arms to them again, her face, pale with a great tenderness, uplifted.

"You, you, you! "she whispered. "I love you!"

And yet it was to nothing definite, to no man, nor outline of a man, to no phantom nor dream-lover, that she spoke; neither to him she had affronted, nor to him who had bidden her look to the stars. Nor was it to the stars themselves.

She returned slowly and thoughtfully to the house, wondering what she had meant.

CHAPTER XI

A VOICE IN A GARDEN

Crailey came home the next day with a new poem, but no fish. He lounged up the stairs, late in the afternoon, humming cheerfully to himself, and, dropping his rod in a corner of Tom's office, laid the poem on the desk before his partner, produced a large, newly-replenished flask, opened it, stretched himself comfortably upon a capacious horse-hair sofa, drank a deep draught, chuckled softly, and requested Mr. Vanrevel to set the rhymes to music immediately.

"Try it on your instrument," he said. "It's a simple verse about nothing but stars, and you can work it out in twenty minutes with the guitar."

"It is broken," said Tom, not looking up from his work.

"Broken! When?"

"Last night."

"Who broke it?"

"It fell from the table in my room."

"How? Easily mended, isn't it?"

"I think I shall not play it soon again."

Crailey swung his long legs off the sofa and abruptly sat upright. "What's this?" he asked gravely.

Tom pushed his papers away from him, rose and went to the dusty window that looked to the west, where, at the end of the long street, the sun was setting behind the ruin of charred timbers on the bank of the shining river.

"It seems that I played once too often," he said.

Crailey was thoroughly astonished. He took a long, affectionate pull at the flask and offered it to his partner.

"No," said Tom, turning to him with a troubled face, "and if I were you, I wouldn't either. These fishing trips of yours—"

"Fishing!" Crailey laughed. "Trips of a poetaster! It's then I write best, and write I will! There's a poem, and a damned good one, too, old preacher, in every gill of whiskey, and I'm the lad that can extract it! Lord! what's better than to be out in the open, all by yourself in the woods, or on the river? Think of the long nights alone with the glory of heaven and a good demijohn. Why, a man's thoughts are like actors performing in the air and all the crowding stars for audience! You know in your soul you'd rather have me out there, going it all by myself, than raising thunder over town. And you know, too, it doesn't tell on me; it doesn't show! You couldn't guess, to save your life, how much I've had to-day, now, could you?"

"Yes," returned the other, "I could."

"Well, well," said Crailey, good-naturedly, "we weren't talking of me." He set down the flask, went to his friend and dropped a hand lightly on his shoulder. "What made you break the guitar? Tell me."

"What makes you think I broke it?" asked his partner sharply.

"Tell me why you did it," said Crailey.

And Tom, pacing the room, told him, while Crailey stood in silence, looking him eagerly in the eye whenever Tom turned his way. The listener interrupted seldom; once it was to exclaim: "But you haven't said why you broke the guitar?"

If thine eye offend thee, pluck it out!' I ought to have cut off the hands that played to her." "And cut your throat for singing to her?"

"She was right!" the other answered, striding up and down the room. "Right—a thousand times! in everything she did. That I should even approach her, was an unspeakable insolence. I had forgotten, and so, possibly, had she, but I had not even been properly introduced to her."

"No, you hadn't, that's true," observed Crailey, reflectively. "You don't seem to have much to reproach her with, Tom."

"Reproach her!" cried the other. "That I should dream she would speak to me or have anything to do with me, was to cast a doubt upon her loyalty as a daughter. She was right, I say! And she did the only thing she could do: rebuked me before them all. No one ever merited what he got more roundly than I deserved that. Who was I, in her eyes, that I should besiege her with my importunities, who but her father's worst enemy?"

Deep anxiety knitted Crailey's brow. "I understood she knew of the quarrel," he said, thoughtfully. "I saw that, the other evening when I helped her out of the crowd. She spoke of it on the way home, I remember; but how did she know that you were Vanrevel? No one in town would be apt to mention you to her."

"No, but she did know, you see."

"Yes," returned Mr. Gray slowly. "So it seems! Probably her father told her to avoid you, and described you so that she recognized you as the man who caught the kitten."

He paused, picked up the flask, and again applied himself to its contents, his eyes peering over the up-tilted vessel at Tom, who continued to pace up and down the length of the office. After a time, Crailey, fumbling in his coat, found a long cheroot, and, as he lit it, inquired casually:

"Do you remember if she addressed you by name?"

"I think not," Tom answered, halting. "What does it matter?"

Crailey drew a deep breath.

"It doesn't," he returned.

"She knew me well enough," said Tom, sadly, as he resumed his sentry-go.

"Yes," repeated Crailey, deliberately. "So it seems; so it seems!" He blew a long stream of smoke out into the air before him, and softly murmured again: " So it seems, so it seems."

Silence fell, broken only by the sound of Tom's footsteps,

until, presently, some one informally shouted his name from the street below. It was only Will Cummings, passing the time of day, but when Tom turned from the window after answering him, Crailey, his poem, and his flask were gone.

That evening Vanrevel sat in the dusty office, driving himself to his work with a sharp goad, for there was a face that came between him and all else in the world, and a voice that sounded always in his ears. But the work was done before he rose from his chair, though he showed a haggard visage as he bent above his candles to blow them out.

It was eleven o'clock; Crailey had not come back, and Tom knew that his light-hearted friend would not return for many hours; and so, having no mind to read, and no belief that he could if he tried, he went out to walk the streets. He went down to the river first, and stood for a little while gazing at the ruins of the two warehouses, and that was like a man with a headache beating his skull against a wall. As he stood on the blackened wharf, he saw how the charred beams rose above him against the sky like a gallows, and it seemed to him that nothing could have been a better symbol, for here he had hanged his self-respect. "Reproach her!" He, who had so displayed his imbecility before her! Had he been her father's best friend, he should have had too great a sense of shame to dare to speak to her after that night when her quiet intelligence had exhibited him to himself, and to all the world, as nought else than a fool—and a noisy one at that!

Suddenly a shudder convulsed him; he struck his open palm across his forehead and spoke aloud, while, from horizon to horizon, the night air grew thick with the whispered laughter of observing hobgoblins:

"And even if there had been no stairway, we could have slid down the hose-line!"

He retraced his steps, a tall, gray figure moving slowly through the blue darkness, and his lips formed the heart-sick shadow of a smile when he found that he had unconsciously turned into Carewe Street. Presently he came to a gap in a hedge, through which he had sometimes stolen to hear the sound of a harp and a girl's voice singing; but he did not enter there tonight, though he paused a moment, his head bowed on his breast.

There came a sound of voices; they seemed to be moving toward the hedge, toward the gap where he stood; one a man's eager, quick, but very musical; the other, a girl's, a rich and clear contralto that passed into Tom's soul like a psalm of rejoicing and like a scimitar of flame. He shivered, and moved away quickly, but not before the man's voice, somewhat louder for the moment, came distinctly from the other side of the hedge:

"After all," said the voice, with a ripple of laughter, "after all, weren't you a little hard on that poor Mr. Gray?"

Tom did not understand, but he knew the voice. It was that of Crailey Gray.

He heard the same voice again that night, and again stood unseen. Long after midnight he was still tramping the streets on his lonely rounds, when he chanced to pass the Rouen House, which hostelry bore, to the uninitiated eye, the appearance of having closed its doors upon all hospitalities for the night, in strict compliance with the law of the city fathers, yet a slender wand of bright light might be discovered underneath the street door of the bar-room.

From within the merry retreat issued an uproar of shouting, raucous laughter and the pounding of glasses on tables, heralding all too plainly the hypocrisy of the landlord, and possibly that of the city fathers also. Tom knew what company was gathered there: gamblers, truckmen, drunken farmers, men from the river steamers making riot while their boats lay at the wharf, with a motley gathering of good-for-nothings of the back-alleys, and tippling clerks from the Main Street stores. There came loud cries for a song, and, in answer, the voice of Crailey rose over the general din, somewhat hoarse, and never so musical when he sang as when he spoke, yet so touching in its dramatic tenderness that soon the noise fell away, and the roisterers sat quietly to listen. It was not the first time Ben Jonson's song had stilled a disreputable company.

"I sent thee late a rosy wreath, Not so much honoring thee, As giving it the hope that there It might not withered be."

Perhaps, just then, Vanrevel would have wished to hear him sing anything in the world rather than that, for on Crailey's lips it carried too much meaning tonight, after the voice in the garden. And Tom lingered no more near the betraying sliver of light beneath the door than he had by the gap in the hedge, but went steadily on his way.

Not far from the hotel he passed a small building brightly lighted and echoing with unusual clamors of industry: the office of the Rouen Journal. The press was going, and Mr. Cummings's thin figure crossed and recrossed the windows, while his voice could be heard energetically bidding his assistants to "Look alive!" so that Tom imagined that something might have happened between the Nueces River and the Rio Grande; but he did not stop to ask the journalist, for he desired to behold the face of none of his friends until he had fought out some things within himself. So he strode on toward nowhere.

Day was breaking when Mr. Gray climbed the stairs to his

room. There were two flights, the ascent of the first of which occupied about half an hour of Crailey's invaluable time; and the second might have taken more of it, or possibly consumed the greater part of the morning, had he received no assistance. But, as he reclined to meditate upon the first landing, another man entered the hallway from without, ascended quickly, and Crailey became pleasantly conscious that two strong hands had lifted him to his feet; and, presently, that he was being borne aloft upon the new-comer's back. It seemed quite a journey, yet the motion was soothing, so he made no effort to open his eyes, until he found himself gently deposited upon the couch in his own chamber, when he smiled amiably, and, looking up, discovered his partner standing over him.

Tom was very pale and there were deep, violet scrawls beneath his eyes. For once in his life he bad come home later than Crailey.

"First time, you know," said Crailey, with difficulty. "You'll admit first time completely incapable? Often needed guiding hand, but never—quite—before."

"Yes," said Tom, quietly, "it is the first time I ever saw you quite finished."

"Think I must be growing old and constitution refuses bear it. Disgraceful to be seen in condition, yet celebration justified. H'rah for the news!" He waved his hand wildly. "Old red, white, and blue! American eagle now kindly proceed to scream! Starspangled banner intends streaming to all the trade winds! Sea to sea! Glorious victories on political thieving exhibition—no, expedition! Everybody not responsible for the trouble to go and get himself patriotically killed!"

"What do you mean?"

"Water!" said the other, feebly. Tom brought the pitcher, and Crailey, setting his hot lips to it, drank long and deeply; then, with his friend's assistance, he tied a heavily moistened towel round his head. "All right very soon and sober again," he muttered, and lay back upon the pillow with eyes tightly closed in an intense effort to concentrate his will. When he opened them again, four or five minutes later, they had marvellously cleared and his look was self-contained and sane.

"Haven't you heard the news?" He spoke much more easily now. "It came at midnight to the Journal."

"No; I've been walking in the country."

"The Mexicans crossed the Rio Grande on the twenty-sixth of last month, captured Captain Thornton and murdered Colonel Crook. That means war is certain."

"It has been certain for a long time," said Tom. "Polk has forced it from the first."

"Then it's a devil of a pity he can't be the only man to die!"

"Have they called for volunteers?" asked Tom, going toward the door.

"No; but if the news is true, they will."

"Yes," said Tom; and as he reached the hallway he paused. "Can I help you to undress?"

"Certainly not!" Crailey sat up, indignantly. "Can't you see that I'm perfectly sober? It was the merest temporary fit, and

I've shaken it off. Don't you see?" He got upon his feet, staggered, but shook himself like a dog coming out of the water, and came to the door with infirm steps.

"You're going to bed, aren't you?" asked Tom. "You'd much better."

"No," answered Crailey. "Are you?

"No. I'm going to work."

"You've been all up night, too, haven't you?" Crailey put his hand on the other's shoulder. "Were you hunting for me?"

"No; not last night."

Crailey lurched suddenly, and Tom caught him about the waist to steady him.

"Sweethearting, tippling, vingt-et-un, or poker, eh, Tom?" he shouted, thickly, with a wild laugh. "Ha, ha, old smug-face, up to my bad tricks at last!" But, recovering himself immediately, he pushed the other off at arm's length, and slapped himself smartly on the brow. "Never mind; all right, all right—only a bad wave, now and then. A walk will make me more a man than ever."

"You'd much better go to bed, Crailey."

"I can't. I'm going to change my clothes and go out."

"Why?"

Crailey did not answer, but at that moment the Catholic church-bell, summoning the faithful to mass, pealed loudly on the morning air; and the steady glance of Tom Vanrevel rested upon the reckless eyes of the man beside him as they listened together to its insistent call. Tom said, gently, almost timidly:

"You have an—engagement?"

This time the answer came briskly. "Yes; I promised to take Fanchon to the cemetery before breakfast, to place some flowers on the grave of the little brother who died. This happens to be his birthday."

It was Tom who averted his eyes, not Crailey.

"Then you'd best hurry," he said, hesitatingly; "I mustn't keep you," and went downstairs to his office with flushed cheeks, a hanging head, and an expression which would have led a stranger to believe that he had just been caught in a lie.

He went to the Main Street window, and seated himself upon the ledge, the only one in the room not too dusty for occupation; for here, at this hour, Tom had taken his place every morning since Elizabeth Carewe had come from the convent. The window was a coign of vantage, commanding the corner of Carewe and Main streets. Some distance west of the corner, the Catholic church cast its long shadow across Main Street, and, in order to enter the church, a person who lived upon Carewe Street must pass the corner, or else make a half-mile detour and approach from the other direction— which the person never did. Tom had thought it out the first night that the image of Miss Betty had kept him awake—and that was the first night Miss Carewe spent in Rouen—the St. Mary's girl would be sure to go to mass every day, which was why the window-ledge was dusted the next morning.

The glass doors of the little corner drug-store caught the early sun of the hot May morning and became like sheets of polished brass; a farmer's wagon rattled down the dusty street; a group of Irish waitresses from the hotel made the boardwalk rattle under their hurried steps as they went toward the church, talking busily to one another; and a blinking youth in his shirt-sleeves, who wore the air of one newly, but not gladly, risen, began to struggle mournfully with the shutters of Madrillon's bank. A moment later, Tom heard Crailey come down the stairs, sure of foot and humming lightly to himself. The door of the office was closed; Crailey did not look in, but presently appeared, smiling, trim, immaculate, all in white linen, on the opposite side of the street, and offered badinage to the boy who toiled at the shutters.

The bell had almost ceased to ring when a lady, dressed plainly in black, but graceful and tall, came rapidly out of Carewe Street, turned at the corner by the little drug-store, and went toward the church. The boy was left staring, for Crailey's banter broke off in the middle of a word.

He overtook her on the church steps, and they went in together.

That afternoon Fanchon Bareaud told Tom how beautiful her betrothed had been to her; he had brought her a great bouquet of violets and lilies-of-the-valley, and had taken her to the cemetery to place them on the grave of her baby brother, whose birthday it was. Tears came to Fanchon's eyes as she spoke of her lover's goodness, and of how wonderfully he had talked as they stood beside the little grave.

"He was the only one who remembered that this was poor tiny Jean's birthday!" she said, and sobbed. "He came just after breakfast and asked me to go out there with him."

CHAPTER XII

THE ROOM IN THE CUPOLA

Mr. Carewe returned, one warm May afternoon, by the six o'clock boat, which was sometimes a day late and sometimes a few hours early; the latter contingency arising, as in the present instance, when the owner was aboard. Nelson drove him from the wharf to the bank, where he conferred briefly, in an undertone, with Eugene Madrillon; after which Eugene sent a note containing three words to Tappingham Marsh. Marsh tore up the note, and sauntered over to the club, where he found General Trumble and Jefferson Bareaud amicably discussing a pitcher of cherry bounce.

"He has come," said Tappingham, pleased to find the pair the only occupants of the place. "He saw Madrillon, and there's a session tonight."

"Praise the Lord!" exclaimed the stout General, rising to his feet. "I'll see old Chenoweth at once. My fingers have the itch."

"And mine, too," said Bareaud. "I'd begun to think we'd never have a go with him again."

"You must see that Crailey comes. We want a full table.

Drag him, if you can't get him any other way."

"He won't need urging," said Jefferson.

"But he cut us last time."

"He won't cut tonight. What hour?"

"Nine," answered Tappingham. "It's to be a full sitting, remember."

"Don't fear for us," laughed Trumble.

"Nor for Crailey," Jefferson added. "After so long a vacation you couldn't keep him away if you chained him to the court-house pillars; he'd tear 'em in two!"

"Here's to our better fortunes, then! said the old soldier, filling a glass for Tappingham; and, "Here's to our better fortunes!" echoed the young men, pouring off the gentle liquor heartily. Having thus made libation to their particular god, the trio separated. But Jefferson did not encounter the alacrity of acceptance he expected from Crailey, when he found him, half an hour later, at the hotel bar. Indeed, at first, Mr. Gray not oniy refused outright to go, but seriously urged the same course upon Jefferson; moreover, his remonstrance was offered in such evident good faith that Bareaud, in the act of swallowing one of his large doses of quinine, paused with only half the powder down his throat, gazing, nonplussed, at his prospective brother-in-law.

"My immortal soul!" he gasped. "Is this Crailey Gray? What's the trouble?"

"Nothing," replied Crailey, quietly. "Only don't go, you've lost enough."

"Well, you're a beautiful one!" Jefferson exclaimed, with an incredulous laugh. "You're a master hand; you, to talk about losing enough!"

"I know, I know," Crailey began, shaking his head, "but—"

"You've promised Fanchon never to go again, and you're afraid Miss Betty will see or hear us, and tell her you were there."

"I don't know Miss Carewe."

"Then you needn't fear; besides, she'll be out when we come, and asleep when we go. She will never know we've been in the house."

"That has nothing to do with it," said Crailey, impatiently; and he was the more earnest because he remembered the dangerous geography of the Carewe house, which made it impossible for anyone to leave the cupola-room except by the long hall which passed certain doors. "I will not go, and what's more, I promised Fanchon I'd try to keep you out of it hereafter."

"Lord, but we're virtuous!" laughed the incredulous Jefferson. "I'll come for you at a quarter to nine."

"I will not go, I tell you."

Jefferson roared. "Yes, you will. You couldn't keep from it if you tried!" And he took himself off, laughing violently, again promising to call for Crailey on his way to the tryst, and leaving him still warmly protesting that it would be a great folly for either of them to go.

Crailey looked after the lad's long, thin figure with an

expression as near anger as he ever wore. "He'll go," he said to himself.

"And—ah, well—I'll have to risk it! I'll go with him, but only to try and bring him away early—that is, as early as it's safe to be sure that they are asleep downstairs. And I won't play. No, I'll not play; I'll not play."

He paid his score and went out of the hotel by a side door. Some distance up the street, Bareaud was still to be seen, lounging homeward in the pleasant afternoon sunshine, he stopped on a corner and serenely poured another quinine powder into himself and threw the paper to a couple of pigs who looked up from the gutter maliciously.

"Confound him!" said Crailey, laughing ruefully. "He makes me a missionary—for I'll keep my word to Fanchon in that, at least! I'll look after Jefferson tonight. Ah, I might as well be old Tom Vanrevel, indeed!"

Meanwhile, Mr. Carewe had taken possession of his own again. His daughter ran to the door to meet him; she was trembling a little, and, blushing and smiling, held out both her hands to him, so that Mrs. Tanberry vowed this was the loveliest creature in the world, and the kindest.

Mr. Carewe bowed slightly, as to an acquaintance, and disregarded the extended hands.

At that, the blush faded from Miss Betty's cheeks; she trembled no more, and a salutation as icy as her father's was returned to him. He bent his heavy brows upon her, and shot a black glance her way, being, of course, immediately enraged by her reflection of his own manner, but he did not speak to her.

Nor did he once address her during the evening meal, preferring to honor Mrs. Tanberry with his conversation, to that diplomatic lady's secret anger, but outward amusement. She cheerfully neglected to answer him at times, having not the slightest awe of him, and turned to the girl instead; indeed, she was only prevented from rating him soundly at his own table by the fear that she might make the situation more difficult for her young charge. As soon as it was possible, she made her escape with Miss Betty, and they drove away in the twilight to pay visits of duty, leaving Mr. Carewe frowning at his coffee on the veranda.

When they came home, three hours later, Miss Betty noticed that a fringe of illumination bordered each of the heavily curtained windows in the cupola, and she uttered an exclamation, for she had never known that room to be lighted.

"Look!" she cried, touching Mrs. Tanberry's arm, as the horses trotted through the gates under a drizzle of rain, "I thought the room in the cupola was empty. It's always locked, and when I came from St. Mary's he told me that old furniture was stored there."

Mrs. Tanberry was grateful for the darkness. "He may have gone there to read," she answered, in a queer voice. "Let us go quietly to bed, child, so as not to disturb him."

Betty had as little desire to disturb her father as she had to see him; therefore she obeyed her friend's injunction, and went to her room on tiptoe. The house was very silent as she lit the candles on her bureau. Outside, the gentle drizzle and the soothing tinkle from the eaves were the only sounds; within, there was but the faint rustle of garments from Mrs. Tanberry's room. Presently the latter ceased to be heard, and a wooden moan of protest from the four-poster upon which the good lady reposed, announced that she had drawn the curtains and wooed the rulers of Nod.

Although it was one of those nights of which they say, "It is a good night to sleep," Miss Betty was not drowsy. She had half-unfastened one small sandal, but she tied the ribbons again, and seated herself by the open window. The ledge and casement framed a dim oblong of thin light from the candles behind her, a lonely lustre, which crossed the veranda to melt shapelessly into darkness on the soggy lawn. She felt a melancholy in the softly falling rain and wet, black foliage that chimed with the sadness of her own spirit. The night suited her very well, for her father's coming had brought a weight of depression with it. Why could he not have spoken one word to her, even a cross one? She knew that he did not love her, yet, merely as a fellow-being, she was entitled to a measure of courtesy; and the fact that she was his daughter could not excuse his failure to render it. Was she to continue to live with him on their present terms? She had no intention to make another effort to alter them; but to remain as they were would be intolerable, and Mrs. Tanberry could not stay forever, to act as a buffer between her and her father. Peering out into the dismal night, she found her own future as black, and it seemed no wonder that the Sisters loved the convent life; that the pale nuns forsook the world wherein there was so much useless unkindness; where women were petty and jealous, like that cowardly Fanchon, and men who looked great were tricksters, like Fanchon's betrothed. Miss Betty clenched her delicate fingers. She would not remember that white, startled face again!

Another face helped her to shut out the recollection: that of the man who had come to mass to meet her yesterday morning, and with whom she had taken a long walk afterward. He had shown her a quaint old English gardener who lived on the bank of the river, had bought her a bouquet, and she had helped him to select another to send to a sick friend. How beautiful the flowers were, and how happy he had made the morning for her, with his gayety, his lightness, and his odd wisdom! Was it only yesterday? Her father's coming had made yesterday a fortnight old.

But the continuously pattering rain and the soft drip-drop from the roof, though as mournful as she chose to find them, began, afterwhile, to weave their somnolent spells, and she slowly drifted from reveries of unhappy sorts, into half-dreams, in which she was still aware she was awake; yet slumber, heavy-eyed, stirring from the curtains beside her with the small night breeze, breathed strange distortions upon familiar things, and drowsy impossibilities moved upon the surface of her thoughts. Her chin, resting upon her hand, sank gently, until her head almost lay upon her relaxed arms.

"That is mine, Crailey Gray!"

She sprang to her feet, immeasurably startled, one hand clutching the back of her chair, the other tremulously pressed to her cheek, convinced that her father had stooped over her and shouted the sentence in her ear. For it was his voice, and the house rang with the words; all the rooms, halls, and even the walls, seemed still murmurous with the sudden sound, like the tingling of a bell after it had been struck. And yet— everything was quiet.

She pressed her fingers to her forehead, trying to untangle the maze of dreams which had evolved this shock for her, the sudden clamor in her father's voice of a name she hated and hoped never to hear again, a name she was trying to forget. But as she was unable to trace anything which had led to it, there remained only the conclusion that her nerves were not what they should be. The vapors having become obsolete for young ladies as an explanation for all unpleasant sensations, they were instructed to have "nerves." This was Miss Betty's first consciousness of her own, and, desiring no greater acquaintance with them, she told herself it was unwholesome to fall asleep in a chair by an open window when the night was as sad as she.

Turning to a chair in front of the small oval mirror of her bureau, she unclasped the brooch. which held her lace collar, and, seating herself, began to unfasten her hair. Suddenly she paused, her uplifted arms falling mechanically to her sides.

Someone was coming through the long hall with a soft, almost inaudible step, a step which was not her father's. She knew at once, with instinctive certainty, that it was not he. Nor was it Nelson, who would have shuffled; nor could it be the vain Mamie, nor one of the other servants, for they did not sleep in the house. It was a step more like a woman's, though certainly it was not Mrs. Tanberry's.

Betty rose, took a candle, and stood silent for a moment, the heavy tresses of her hair, half-unloosed, falling upon her neck and left shoulder like the folds of a dark drapery.

At the slight rustle of her rising, the steps ceased instantly. Her heart set up a wild beating and the candle shook in her hand. But she was brave and young, and, following an irresistible impulse, she ran across the room, flung open the door, and threw the light of the candle into the hall, holding it at arm's length before her.

She came almost face to face with Crailey Gray.

The blood went from his cheeks as a swallow flies down from a roof; he started back against the opposite wall with a stifled groan, while she stared at him blankly, and grew as deathly pale as he.

He was a man of great resource in all emergencies which required a quick tongue, but, for the moment, this was beyond him. He felt himself lost, toppling backward into an abyss, and the uselessness of his destruction made him physically sick. For he need not have been there; he had not wished to come; he had well counted the danger to himself, and this one time in his life had gone to the cupola-room out of good-nature. But Bareaud had been obstinate and Crailey had come away alone, hoping that Jefferson might follow. And here he was, poor trapped rat, convicted and ruined because of a good action! At last he knew consistency to be a jewel, and that a greedy boy should never give a crust; that a fool should stick to his folly, a villain to his deviltry, and each hold his own; for the man who thrusts a good deed into a life of lies is wound about with perilous passes, and in his devious ways a thousand unexpected damnations spring.

Beaten, stunned, hang-jawed with despair, he returned her long, dumfounded gaze hopelessly and told the truth like an inspired dunce.

"I came—I came—to bring another man away," he whispered brokenly; and, at the very moment, several heavy, half-suppressed voices broke into eager talk overhead.

The white hand that held the candle wavered, and the shadows glided in a huge, grotesque dance. Twice she essayed to speak before she could do so, at the same moment motioning him back, for he had made a vague gesture toward her.

"I am not faint. Do you mean, away from up there?" She pointed to the cupola-stairs.

"Yes."

"Have-have you seen my father?"

The question came out of such a depth of incredulousness that it was more an articulation of the lips than a sound, but he caught it; and, with it not hope, but the shadow of a shadow of hope, a hand waving from the far shore to the swimmer who has been down twice. Did she fear for his sake?

"No—I have not seen him." He was groping blindly.

"You did not come from that "

"How did you enter the house?"

The draught through the hall was blowing upon him; the double doors upon the veranda had been left open for coolness. "There," he said, pointing to them.

"But—I heard you come from the other direction."

He was breathing quickly; he saw his chance—if Jefferson Bareaud did not come now.

"You did not hear me come down the stairs." He leaned toward her, risking it all on that.

"Ah!" A sigh too like a gasp burst from Crailey. His head lifted a little, and his eyes were luminous with an eagerness that was almost anguish. He set his utmost will at work to collect himself and to think hard and fast.

"I came here resolved to take a man away, come what would!" he said. "I found the door open, went to the foot of that stairway; then I stopped. I remembered something; I turned, and was going away when you opened the door."

"You remembered what?"

Her strained attitude did not relax, nor, to his utmost scrutiny, was the complete astonishment of her distended gaze altered one whit, but a hint of her accustomed high color was again upon her cheek and her lip trembled a little, like that of a child about to weep. The flicker of hope in his breast increased prodigiously, and the rush of it took the breath from his throat and choked him. Good God! was she going to believe him?

"I remembered—you!"

"What?" she said, wonderingly.

Art returned with a splendid bound, full-pinioned, his beautiful and treacherous Familiar who had deserted him at the crucial instant; but she made up for it now, folding him in protective wings and breathing through his spirit. In rapid and vehement whispers he poured out the words upon the girl in the doorway.

"I have a friend, and I would lay down my life to make him what he could be. He has always thrown everything away, his life, his talents, all his money and all of mine, for the sake of—throwing them away! Some other must tell you about that room; but it has ruined my friend. Tonight I discovered that he had been summoned here, and I made up my mind to come and take him away. Your father has sworn to shoot me if I set foot in his house or on ground of his. Well, my duty was clear and I came to do it. And yet—I stopped at the foot of the stair—because—because I remembered that you were Robert Carewe's daughter. What of you, if I went up and harm came to me from your father? For I swear I would not have touched him! You asked me not to speak of 'personal' things, and I have obeyed you; but you see I must tell you one thing now: I have cared for this friend of mine more than for all else under heaven, but I turned and left him to his ruin, and would a thousand times, rather than bring trouble upon you! 'A thousand times?' Ah! I swear it should be a thousand times a thousand!"

He had paraded in one speech from the prisoner's dock to Capulet's garden, and her eyes were shining into his like a great light when he finished.

"Go quickly," she whispered. "Go quickly! Go quickly!"

"But do you understand?"

"Not yet, but I shall. Will you go? They might come-my father might come-at any moment."

"But—"

"Do you want to drive me quite mad? Please go!" She laid a trembling, urgent hand upon his sleeve.

"Never, until you tell me that you understand," replied Crailey firmly, listening keenly for the slightest sound from overhead. "Never—until then!"

"When I do I shall tell you; now I only know that you must go."

"But tell me - "

"You must go!"

There was a shuffling of chairs on the floor overhead, and Crailey went. He went even more hastily than might have been expected from the adamantine attitude he had just previously assumed. Realizing this as he reached the wet path, he risked stealing round to her window:

"For your sake! "he breathed; and having thus forestalled any trifling imperfection which might arise in her recollection of his exit from the house, he disappeared, kissing his hand to the rain as he ran down the street.

Miss Betty locked her door and pulled close the curtains of her window. A numerous but careful sound of footsteps came from the hall, went by her door and out across the veranda. Silently she waited until she heard her father go alone to his room.

She took the candle and went in to Mrs. Tanberry. She set the light upon a table, pulled a chair close to the bedside, and placed her cool hand lightly on the great lady's forehead.

"Isn't it very late, child? Why are you not asleep?"

"Mrs. Tanberry, I want to know why there was a light in the cupola-room tonight?"

"What?" Mrs. Tanberry rolled herself as upright as possible, and sat with blinking eyes.

"I want to know what I am sure you know, and what I am sure everybody knows, except me. What were they doing there tonight, and what was the quarrel between Mr. Vanrevel and my father that had to do with Mr. Gray?"

Mrs. Tanberry gazed earnestly into the girl's face. After a long time she said in a gentle voice:

"Child, has it come to matter that much?"

"Yes," said Miss Betty.

CHAPTER XIII

THE TOCSIN

Tom Vanrevel always went to the post-office soon after the morning distribution of the mail; that is to say, about ten o'clock, and returned with the letters for the firm of Gray and Vanrevel, both personal and official. Crailey and he shared everything, even a box at the post-office; and in front of this box, one morning, after a night of rain, Tom stood staring at a white envelope bearing a small, black seal. The address was in a writing he had never seen before, but the instant it fell under his eye he was struck with a distinctly pleasurable excitement.

Whether through some spiritual exhalation of the writer fragrant on any missive, or because of a hundred microscopic impressions, there are analysts who are able to select, from a pile of letters written by women (for the writing of women exhibits certain phenomena more determinably than that of men) those of the prettiest or otherwise most attractive. And out upon the lover who does not recognize his mistress's hand at the first glimpse ever he has of it, without post-mark or other information to aid him! Thus Vanrevel, worn, hollow-eyed, and sallow, in the Rouen post-office, held the one letter separate from a dozen (the latter not, indeed, from women), and stared at it until a little color came back to his dark skin and a great deal of brightness to his eye. He was no analyst of handwritings, yet it came to him instantly that this note was from a pretty woman. To see that it was from a woman was simple, but that he knew—and he did know—that she was pretty, savors of the occult. More than this: there was something about it that thrilled him. Suddenly, and without reason, he knew that it came from Elizabeth Carewe.

He walked back quickly to his office with the letter in the left pocket of his coat, threw the bundle of general correspondence upon his desk, went up to the floor above, and paused at his own door to listen. Deep breathing from across the hall indicated that Mr. Gray's soul was still encased in slumber, and great was its need, as Tom had found his partner, that morning at five, stretched upon the horsehair sofa in the office, lamenting the emptiness of a bottle which had been filled with fiery Bourbon in the afternoon.

Vanrevel went to his own room, locked the door, and took the letter from his pocket. He held it between his fingers carefully, as though it were alive and very fragile, and he looked at it a long time, holding it first in one hand, then in the other, before he opened it. At last, however, after examining all the blades of his pocketknife, he selected one brighter than the others, and loosened the flap of the envelope as gently and carefully as if it had been the petal of a rose-bud that he was opening.

"Dear Mr. Vanrevel: "I believed you last night, though I did not understand. But I understand, now—everything—and, bitter to me as the truth is, I must show you plainly that I know all of it, nor can I rest until I do show you. I want you to answer this letter—though I must not see you again for a long time—and in your answer you must set me right if I am anywhere mistaken in what I have learned.

"At first, and until after the second time we met, I did not believe in your heart, though I did in your mind and humor. Even since then, there have come strange, small, inexplicable mistrustings of you, but now I throw them all away and trust you wholly, Monsieur Citizen Georges Meilbac!—I shall always think of you in those impossible garnishments of my poor great-uncle, and I persuade myself that he must have been a little like you.

"I trust you because I have heard the story of your profound goodness. The first reason for my father's dislike was your belief in freedom as the right of all men. Ah, it is not your pretty exaggerations and flatteries (I laugh at them!) that speak for you, but your career, itself, and the brave things you have done. My father's dislike flared into hatred because you worsted him when he discovered that he could not successfully defend the wrong against you and fell back upon sheer insult.

"He is a man whom I do not know—strange as that seems as I write it. It is only to you, who have taught me so much, that I could write it. I have tried to know him and to realize that I am his daughter, but we are the coldest acquaintances, that is all; and I cannot see how a change could come. I do not understand him; least of all do I understand why he is a gambler. It has been explained to me that it is his great passion, but all I comprehend in these words is that they are full of shame for his daughter.

"This is what was told me: he has always played heavily and skillfully—adding much to his estate in that way—and in Rouen always with a certain coterie, which was joined, several years ago, by the man you came to save last night.

"Your devotion to Mr. Gray has been the most beautiful thing in your life. I know all that the town knows of that, except the thousand hidden sacrifices you have made for him, those things which no one will ever know. (And yet, you see, I know them after all!) For your sake, because you love him, I will not even call him unworthy.

"I have heard—from one who told unwillingly—the story of the night two years ago, when the play ran so terribly high; and how, in the morning when they went away, all were poorer except one, their host!—how Mr. Gray had nothing left in the world, and owed my father a great sum which was to be paid in twenty-four hours; how you took everything you had saved in the years of hard work at your profession, and borrowed the rest on your word, and brought it to my father that afternoon; how, when you had paid your friend's debt, you asked my father not to play with Mr. Gray again; and my father made that his excuse to send you a challenge. You laughed at the challenge—and you could afford to laugh at it.

"But this is all shame, shame for Robert Carewe's daughter. It seems to me that I should hide and not lift my head; that I, being of my father's blood, could never look you in the face again. It is so unspeakably painful and ugly. I think of my father's stiff pride and his look of the eagle,—and he still plays with your friend, almost always 'successfully!' And your friend still comes to play!—but I will not speak of that side of it

"Mr. Gray has made you poor, but I know it was not that which made you come seeking him last night, when I found you there in the hail. It was for his sake you came—and you went away for mine. Now that I know, at last—now that I have heard what your life has been (and oh I heard so much more than I have written!)—now that my eyes have been opened to see you as you are, I am proud, and glad and humble that I can believe that you felt a friendship for me strong enough to have made you go 'for my sake.' You will write to me just once, won't you? and tell me if there was any error in what I listened to; but you must not come to the garden. Now that I know you, I cannot meet you clandestinely again. It would hurt the dignity which I feel in you now, and my own poor dignity—such as it is! I have been earnestly warned of the danger to you. Besides, you must let me test myself. I am all fluttering and frightened and excited. You will obey me, won't you ?—do not come until I send for you. Elizabeth Carewe."

Mr. Gray, occupied with his toilet about noon, heard his partner descending to the office with a heavy step, and issued from his room to call a hearty greeting. Tom looked back over his shoulder and replied cheerily, though with a certain embarrassment; but Crailey, catching sight of his face, uttered a sharp ejaculation and came down to him.

"Why, what's the matter, Tom? You're not going to be sick? You look like the devil and all!"

"I'm all right, never fear!" Tom laughed, evading the other's eye. "I'm going out in the country on some business, and I dare say I shall not be back for a couple of days; it will be all up and down the county." He set down a travelling-bag he was carrying, and offered the other his hand. "Good-by."

"Can't I go for you? You don't look able "

"No, no. It's something I'll have to attend to myself."

"Ah, I suppose," said Crailey, gently, "I suppose it's important, and you couldn't trust me to handle it. Well—God knows you're right! I've shown you often enough how incompetent I am to do anything but write jingles!"

"You do some more of them—without the whiskey, Crailey. They're worth more than all the lawing Gray and Vanrevel have ever done or ever will do. Good-by—and be kind to yourself."

He descended to the first landing, and then, "Oh, Crailey," he called, with the air of having forgotten something he had meant to say.

"Yes, Tom?"

"This morning at the post-office I found a letter addressed to me. I opened it and—" He hesitated, and uneasily shifted his weight from one foot to the other, with a feeble, deprecatory laugh.

"Yes, what of it?"

"Well—there seemed to be a mistake. I think it must have been meant for you. Somehow, she—she's picked up a good many wrong impressions, and, Lord knows how, but she's mixed our names up and—and I've left the letter for you. It's on my table."

He turned and calling a final good-by over his shoulder, went clattering noisily down to the street and vanished from Crailey's sight.

Noon found Tom far out on the National Road, creaking along over the yellow dust in a light wagon, between bordering forests that smelt spicily of wet underbrush and May-apples; and, here and there, when they would emerge from the woods to cleared fields, liberally outlined by long snake-fences of black walnut, the steady, jog-trotting old horse lifted his head and looked interested in the world, but Tom never did either. Habitually upright, walking or sitting, straight, keen, and alert, that day's sun saw him drearily hunched over, mile after mile, his forehead laced with lines of pain. He stopped at every farm-house and cabin, and, where the young men worked in the fields, hailed them from the road, or hitched his horse to the fence and crossed the soft furrows to talk with them. At such times he stood erect again, and spoke stirringly, finding eager listeners. There was one question they asked him over and over:

"But are you sure the call will come?"

"As sure as that we stand here; and it will come before the week is out. We must be ready!"

Often, when he left them, they would turn from the work in hand, leaving it as it was, to lie unfinished in the fields, and make their way slowly and thoughtfully to their homes, while Tom climbed into his creaking little wagon once more, only to fall into the same dull, hunched-over attitude. He had many things to think out before he faced Rouen and Crailey Gray again, and more to fight through to the end with himself. Three days he took for it, three days driving through the soft May weather behind the kind, old jog-trotting horse; three days on the road, from farm-house to farm-house and from field to field, from cabin of the woods to cabin in the clearing. Tossing unhappily at night, he lay sleepless till dawn, though not because of the hard beds; and when daylight came, journeyed steadily on again, over the vagabond little hills that had gypsied it so far into the prairie-land in their wanderings from their range on the Ohio, and, passing the hills, went on through the flat forest-land, always hunched over dismally in the creaking wagon.

But on the evening of the third day he drove into town, with the stoop out of his shoulders and the lustre back in his eyes. He was haggard, gray, dusty, but he had solved his puzzle, and one thing was clear in his mind as the thing that he would do. He patted the old horse a hearty farewell as he left him with the liveryman from whom be had hired him, and strode up Main Street with the air of a man who is going somewhere. It was late, but there were more lights than usual in the windows and more people on the streets. Boys ran shouting, while, here and there, knots of men argued loudly, and in front of the little corner drug-store a noisily talkative, widely gesticulative crowd of fifty or more had gathered. An old man, a cobbler, who had left a leg at Tippecanoe and replaced it with a wooden one, chastely decorated with designs of his own carving, came stumping excitedly down the middle of the street, where he walked for fear of the cracks in the wooden pavement, which were dangerous to his art-leg when he came from the Rouen House bar, as on the present occasion. He hailed Tom by name.

"You're the lad, Tom Vanrevel," he shouted. "You're the man to lead the boys out for the glory of the State! You git the whole blame Fire Department out and enlist 'em before morning! Take 'em down to the Rio Grande, you hear me?

And you needn't be afraid of their puttin' it out, if it ketches afire, neither!"

Tom waved his hand and passed on; but at the open doors of the Catholic Church he stopped and looked up and down the street, and then, unnoticed, entered to the dim interior, where the few candles showed only a bent old woman in black kneeling at the altar. Tom knew where Elizabeth Carewe knelt each morning; he stepped softly through the shadowy silence to her place, knelt, and rested his head upon the rail of the bench before him.

The figure at the altar raised itself after a time, and the old woman limped slowly up a side aisle, mumbling her formulas, courtesying to the painted saints, on her way out. The very thinnest lingerings of incense hung on the air, seeming to Tom like the faint odor that might exhale from a heavy wreath of marguerites, worn in dark-brown hair. Yet, the place held nothing but peace and good-will. And he found nothing else in his own heart. The street was quiet when he emerged from that lorn vigil; the corner groups had dissolved; shouting youths no longer patrolled the sidewalks. Only one quarter showed signs of life: the little clubhouse, where the windows still shown brightly, and whence came the sound of many voices settling the destinies of the United States of America. Thither Tom bent his steps, thoughtfully, and with a quiet mind. There was a small veranda at the side of the house; here he stood unobserved to look in upon his noisy and agitated friends.

They were all there, from the old General and Mr. Bareaud, to the latter's son, Jefferson, and young Frank Chenoweth. They were gathered about a big table upon which stood a punch-bowl and Trumble, his brow as angry red as the liquor in the cup he held, was proposing a health to the President in a voice of fury.

"In spite of all the Crailey Grays and traitors this side of hell!" he finished politely.

Crailey emerged instantaneously from the general throng and mounted a chair, tossing his light hair back from his forehead, his eyes sparkling and happy. "You find your own friends already occupying the place you mentioned, do you, General?" he asked.

General Trumble stamped and shook his fist.

"You're a spawn of Aaron Burr!" he vociferated. "There's not a man here to stand by your infernal doctrines. You sneer at your own State, you sneer at your own country, you defile the sacred ground! What are you, by the Almighty, who attack your native land in this, her hour of peril!"

"Peril to my native land!" laughed Crailey. "From Santa Anna?"

"The General's right, sir," exclaimed the elder Chenoweth indignantly, and most of the listeners appeared to agree with him. "It's a poor time to abuse the President when he's called for volunteers and our country is in danger, sir!"

"Who is in danger?" answered Crailey, lifting his hand to still the clamor of approbation that arose. "Is Polk in danger? Or Congress? But that would be too much to hope! Do you expect to see the Greasers in Washington? No, you idiots, you don't! Yet there'll be plenty of men to suffer and die; and the first should be those who thrust this war on us and poor little Mexico; but it won't be they; the men who'll do the fighting and dying will be the country boys and the like of us from the towns, while Mr. Polk sits planning at the White House how he can get elected again. I wish Tom were here, confound you! You listen to him because he always has the facts and I'm just an embroiderer, you think. What's become of the gaudy campaign cry you were all wearing your lungs out with a few months ago? 'Fifty-four-forty or fight!' Bah! Polk twisted the lion's tail with that until after election. Then he saw he had to make you forget it, or fight England and be ruined, so he forces war on Mexico, and the country does forget it. That's it: he asks three regiments of volunteers from this State to die of fevers and get shot, so that he can steal another country and make his own elect him again. And you ask me to drink the health of the politician who sits at home and sends his fellowmen to die to fix his rotten jobs for him?" Crailey had persuaded himself into such earnestness, that the depth of his own feeling almost choked him, but he finished roundly in his beautiful, strong voice: "I'll drink for the good punch's sake—but that health ?—I'll see General Trumble in heaven before I'll drink it!"

There rose at once a roar of anger and disapproval, and Crailey became a mere storm centre amid the upraised hands gestulating madly at him as he stood, smiling again, upon his chair.

"This comes of living with Tom Vanrevel!" shouted the General furiously. "This is his damned Abolition teaching! You're only his echo; you spend half your life playing at being Vanrevel!"

"Where is Vanrevel?" said Tappingham Marsh.

"Ay, where is he!" raged Trumble, hammering the table till the glasses rang. "Let him come and answer for his own teaching; it's wasted time to talk to this one; he's only the pupil. Where is the traitor?"

"Here," answered a voice from the doorway; and though the word was spoken quietly it was nevertheless, at that juncture, silencing. Everyone turned toward the door as Vanrevel entered. But the apoplectic General, whom Crailey's speech had stirred to a fury beyond control, almost leaped at Tom's thoat.

"Here's the tea-sipping old Granny," he bellowed hoarsely. (He was ordinarily very fond of Tom.) "Here's the master! Here's the man whose example teaches Crailey Gray to throw mud at the flag. He'll stay here at home with Crailey, of course, and throw more, while the others boys march out to die under it."

"On the contrary, answered Tom, raising his voice, "I think you'll find Crailey Gray the first to enlist, and as for myself, I've raised sixty men in the country, and I want forty more from Rouen, in order to offer the Governor a full company. So it's come to 'the King, not the man'; Polk is a pitiful trickster, but the country needs her sons; that's enough for us to know; and while I won't drink to James Polk "—he plunged a cup in the bowl and drew it out brimming—"I'll empty this to the President!"

It was then that from fifty throats the long, wild shout went up that stirred Rouen, and woke the people from their midnight beds for half a mile around.

CHAPTER XIV

THE FIRM OF GRAY AND VANREVEL

For the first time it was Crailey who sat waiting for Tom to come home. In a chair drawn to his partner's desk in the dusty office, he half-reclined, arms on the desk, his chin on his clenched fists. To redeem the gloom he had lit a single candle, which painted him dimly against the complete darkness of his own shadow, like a very old portrait whose background time has solidified into shapeless browns; the portrait of a fair-haired gentleman, the cavalier, or the Marquis, one might have said at first glance; not describing it immediately as that of a poet, for there was no mark of art upon Crailey, not even in his hair, for they all wore it rather long then. Yet there was a mark upon him, never more vivid than as he sat waiting in the loneliness of that night for Tom Vanrevel; though what the mark was and what its significance might have been puzzling to define. Perhaps, after all, Fanchon Bareaud had described it best when she told Crailey one day, with a sudden hint of apprehensive tears, that he had a "look of fate."

Tom took his own time in coming; he had stayed at the club to go over his lists—so he had told Crailey—with the General and old Bareaud. His company was almost complete, and Crailey had been the first to volunteer, to the dumfounding of Trumble, who had proceeded to drink his health again and again. But the lists could not detain Tom two hours, Crailey knew, and it was two hours since the new volunteers had sung "The Star Spangled Banner" over the last of the punch, and had left the club to Tom and the two old men. Only once or twice in that time had Crailey shifted his position, or altered the direction of his set gaze at nothing. But at last he rose, went to the window and, leaning far out, looked down the street toward the little clubhouse. Its lights were extinguished and all was dark up and down the street. Abruptly Crailey went back to the desk and blew out the candle, after which he sat down again in the same position. Twenty minutes later he heard Tom's step on the stair, coming up very softly. Crailey waited in silence until his partner reached the landing, then relit the candle.

"Tom," he called. "Come in, please, I've been waiting for you."

There was a pause before Tom answered from the hall:

"I'm very tired, Crailey. I think I'll go up to bed."

"No," said Crailey, "come in."

The door was already open, but Tom turned toward it reluctantly. He stopped at the threshold and the two looked at each other.

"I thought you wouldn't come as long as you believed I was up," said Crailey, " so I blew out the light. I'm sorry I kept you outside so long."

"Crailey, I'm going away to-morrow," the other began. "I am to go over and see the Governor and offer him this company, and to-night I need sleep, so please-

"No," interrupted Crailey quietly, "I want to know what you're going to do."

"To do about what?"

"About me."

"Oh!" Tom's eyes fell at once from his friend's face and rested upon the floor. Slowly he walked to the desk and stood in embarrassed contemplation of the littered books and papers, while the other waited.

"I think it's best for you to tell me," said Crailey.

"You think so?" Tom's embarrassment increased visibly, and there was mingled with it an odd appearance of apprehension, probably to relieve which he very deliberately took two long cheroots from his pocket, laid one on the desk for Crailey and lit the other himself, with extreme carefulness, at the candle. After this ceremonial he dragged a chair to the window, tilted back in it with his feet on the low sill, his back to the thin light and his friend, and said in a slow, gentle tone: "Well, Crailey?"

"I suppose you mean that I ought to offer my explanation first," said the other, still standing. "Well, there isn't any." He did not speak doggedly or sullenly, as one in fault, but more with the air of a man curiously ready to throw all possible light upon a cloudy phenomenon. "It's very simple—all that I know about it. I went there first on the evening of the Madrillon masquerade and played a little comedy for her, so that some of my theatrical allusions—they weren't very illuminating!—to my engagement to Fanchon, made her believe I was Vanrevel when her father told her about the pair of us. I discovered that the night his warehouses burned—and I saw something more, because I can't help seeing such things: that yours was just the character to appeal to a young girl fresh from the convent and full of honesty and fine dreams and fire. Nobody could arrange a more fatal fascination for a girl of nineteen than to have a deadly quarrel with her father. And that's especially true when the father's like that mad brute of a Bob Carewe! Then, too, you're more or less the town model of virtue and popular hero, in spite of the Abolitionism, just as I am the town scamp. So I let it go on, and played a little at being you, saying the things that you only think—that was all. It isn't strange that it's lasted until now, not more than three weeks, after all. She's only seen you four or five times, and me not much oftener. No one speaks of you to her, and I've kept out of sight when others were about. Mrs. Tanberry is her only close friend, and, naturally, wouldn't be apt to mention that you are dark and I am fair, or to describe us personally, any more than you and I would mention the general appearance of people we both meet about town. But you needn't tell me that it can't last much longer. Some petty, unexpected trifle will turn up, of course. All that I want to know is what you mean to do."

"To do?" repeated Tom softly, and blew a long scarf of smoke out of the window.

"Ah!" Crailey's voice grew sharp and loud. "There are many things you needn't tell me! You need not tell me what I've done to you—nor what you think of me! You need not tell me that you have others to consider, that you have Miss Carewe to think of. Don't you suppose I know that? And you need not tell me that you have a duty to Fanchon—"

"Yes," Tom broke in, his tone not quite steady. "Yes, I've thought of that."

"Well?"

"Have you—did you—" he hesitated, but Crailey understood immediately.

"No; I haven't seen her again."

"But you—"

"Yes—I wrote. I answered the letter."

"As-"

"Yes; I signed your name. I told you that I had just let things go on," Crailey answered, with an impatient movement of his hands. "What are you going to do?"

"I'm going over to see the Governor in the morning. I'll be away two or three days, I imagine."

"Vanrevel!" exclaimed Crailey hotly, "Will you give me an answer and not beat about the bush any longer? Or do you mean that you refuse to answer?"

Tom dropped his cigar upon the brick window-ledge with an abysmal sigh. "Oh, no, it isn't that," he answered mildly "I've been thinking it all over for three days in the country, and when I got back tonight I found that I had come to a decision without knowing it, and that I had come to it even before I started; my leaving the letter for you proved it. It's a little like this Mexican war, a mixed-up problem and only one thing clear. A few schemers have led the country into it to increase the slave-power and make us forget that we threatened England when we couldn't carry out the threat. And yet, if you look at it broadly, these are the smaller things and they do not last. The means by which the country grows may be wrong, but its growth is right; it is only destiny, working out through lies and blood, but the end will be good.

It is bound to happen and you can't stop it. I believe the men who make this war for their own uses will suffer in hell-fire for it; but it is made, and there's only one thing I can see as the thing for me to do. They've called me every name on earth—and the same with you, too, Crailey—because I'm an Abolitionist, but now, whether the country has sinned or not, a good many thousand men have got to do the bleeding for her, and I want to be one of them. That's the one thing that is plain to me."

"Yes," returned Crailey. "You know I'm with you; and I think you're always right. Yes; we'll all be on the way in a fortnight or so. Do you mean you won't quarrel with me because of that? Do you mean it would be a poor time now, when we're all going out to take our chances together?"

"Quarrel with you!" Tom rose and came to the desk, looking across it at his friend. "Did you think I might do that?"

"Yes—I thought so."

"Crailey!" And now Tom's expression showed desperation; it was that of a man whose apprehensions have culminated and who is forced to face a crisis long expected, long averted, but imminent at last. His eyes fell from Crailey's clear gaze and his hand fidgeted among the papers on the desk.

"No," he began with a painful lameness and hesitation. "I did not mean it—no; I meant, that, in the same way, only one thing in this other—this other affair that seems so confused and is such a problem—only one thing has grown clear. It doesn't seem to me that—that—" here he drew a deep breath, before he went on with increasing nervousness—" that if you like a man and have lived with him a good many years; that is to say, if you're really much of a friend to him, I don't believe you sit on a high seat and judge him. Judging, and all that, haven't much part in it. And it seems to me that you've got yourself into a pretty bad mix-up, Crailey."

"Yes," said Crailey. "It's pretty bad."

"Well," Tom looked up now, with an almost tremulous smile, "I believe that is about all I can make of it. Do you think it's the part of your best friend to expose you? It seems to me that if there ever was a time when I ought to stand by you, it's now."

There was a silence while they looked at each other across the desk in the faint light. Tom's eye fell again as Crailey opened his lips.

"And in spite of everything," Crailey said breathlessly, "you mean that you won't tell?"

"How could I, Crailey?" said Tom Vanrevel as be turned away.

CHAPTER XV

WHEN JUNE CAME

"Methought I met a Damsel Fair And tears were in her eyes; Her head and arms were bare, I heard her bursting sighs.

"I stopp'd and looked her in the face, 'Twas then she sweetly smiled. Her features shone with mournful grace, Far more than Nature's child.

"With diffident and downcast eye, In modest tones she spoke; She wiped a tear and gave a sigh, And then her silence broke—"

So sang Mrs. Tanberry at the piano, relieving the melancholy which possessed her; but Nelson, pausing in the hail to listen, and exceedingly curious concerning the promised utterance of the Damsel Fair, was to suffer disappointment, as the ballad was broken off abruptly and the songstress closed the piano with a monstrous clatter. Little doubt may be entertained that the noise was designed to disturb Mr. Carewe, who sat upon the veranda consulting a brown Principe, and less that the intended insult was accomplished. For an expression of a vindictive nature was precipitated in that quarter so simultaneously that the bang of the pianolid and the curse were even as the report of a musket and the immediate cry of the wounded.

Mrs. Tanberry at once debouched upon the piazza, showing a vast, clouded countenance. "And I hope to heaven you already had a headache!" she exclaimed.

"The courtesy of your wish, madam," Carewe replied, with an angry flash of his eye, "is only equaled by the kindness of heaven in answering it. I have, in fact, a headache. I always have, nowadays."

"That's good news," returned the lady heartily.

"I thank you," retorted her host.

"Perhaps if you treated your daughter even a decent Indian's kind of politeness, you'd enjoy better health."

"Ah! And in what failure to perform my duty toward her have I incurred your displeasure?"

"Where is she now?" exclaimed the other excitably. "Where is she now?"

"I cannot say."

"Yes, you can, Robert Carewe!" Mrs. Tanberry retorted, with a wrathful gesture. "You know well enough she's in her own room, and so do I—for I tried to get in to comfort her when I heard her crying. She's in there with the door bolted, where you drove her!"

"I drove her!" he sneered.

"Yes, you did, and I heard you. Do you think I couldn't hear you raging and storming at her like a crazy man? When you get in a temper do you dream there's a soul in the neighborhood who doesn't know it? You're a fool if you do, because they could have heard you swearing down on Main Street, if they'd listened. What are you trying to do to her?— break her spirit?—or what? Because you'll do it, or kill her. I never heard anybody cry so heart-brokenly." Here the good woman's own eyes filled. "What's the use of pretending?" she went on sorrowfully. "You haven't spoken to her kindly since you came home. Do you suppose I'm blind to that? You weren't a bad husband to the poor child's mother; why can't you be a good father to her?"

"Perhaps you might begin by asking her to be a good daughter to me."

"What has she done?"

"The night before I went away she ran to a fire and behaved there like a common street hoyden. The ladies of the Carewe family have not formerly acquired a notoriety of that kind."

"Bah!" said Mrs. Tanberry.

"The next morning, when I taxed her with it, she dutifully defied and insulted me."

"I can imagine the delicacy with which you 'taxed' her. What has that to do with your devilish tantrums of this afternoon, Robert Carewe?"

"I am obliged to you for the expression," he returned. "When I came home, this afternoon, I found her reading that thing." He pointed to many very small fragments of Mr. Cummings's newspaper, which were scattered about the lawn near the veranda. "She was out here, reading an article which I had read downtown and which appeared in a special edition of that rotten sheet, sent out two hours ago."

"Well?"

"Do you know what that article was, madam, do you know what it was?" Although breathing heavily, Mr. Carewe had compelled himself to a certain outward calmness, but now, in the uncontrollable agitation of his anger, he sprang to his feet and struck one of the wooden pillars of the porch a shocking blow with the bare knuckles of his clenched hand. "Do you know what it was? It was a eulogy of that damned Vanrevel! It pretended to be an account of the enrollment of his infernal company, but it was nothing more than a glorification of that nigger-loving hound! His company—a lot of sneaks, who'll run like sheep from the first Greaser—elected him captain yesterday, and today he received an appointment as major! It dries the blood in my veins to think of it!—that black dog a major! Good God! am I never to hear the last of him? Cummings wrote it, the fool, the lying, fawning, slobbering fool; he ought to be shot for it! Neither he nor his paper ever enter my doors again! And I took the dirty sheet from her hands and tore it to pieces—"

"Yes," interposed Mrs. Tanberry, "it looks as if you had done it with your teeth."

"—And stamped it into the ground!"

"Oh, I heard you!" she said.

Carewe came close to her, and gave her a long look from such bitter eyes that her own fell before them. "If you've been treacherous to me, Jane Tanberry," he said, "then God punish you! If they've met—my daughter and that man— while I was away, it is on your head. I don't ask you, because I believe if you knew anything you'd lie for her sake. But I tell you that as she read that paper, she did not hear my step on the walk nor know that I was there until I leaned over her shoulder. And I swear that I suspect her."

He turned and walked to the door, while the indomitable Mrs. Tanberry, silenced for once, sank into the chair he had vacated. Before he disappeared within the house, he paused.

"If Mr. Vanrevel has met my daughter," he said, in a thick voice, stretching out both hands in a strange, menacing gesture toward the town that lay darkling in the growing dusk, "if he has addressed one word to her, or so much as allowed his eyes to rest on her overlong, let him take care of himself!"

"Oh, Robert, Robert," Mrs. Tanberry cried, in a frightened whisper to herself, "all the fun and brightness went out of the world when you came home!"

For, in truth, the gayety and light-heartedness which, during the great lady's too brief reign, had seemed a vital adjunct of the house to make the place resound with music and laughter, were now departed. No more did Mrs. Tanberry extemporize Dan Tuckers, mazourkas, or quadrilles in the ball-room, nor Blind-Man's Buff in the library; no more did serenaders nightly seek the garden with instrumental plunkings and vocal gifts of harmony. Even the green bronze boy of the fountain seemed to share the timidity of the other youths of the town where Mr. Carewe was concerned, for the goblet he held aloft no longer sent a lively stream leaping into the sunshine in translucent gambols, but dribbled and dripped upon him like a morbid autumn rain. The depression of the place was like a drape of mourning purple; but not that house alone lay glum, and there were other reasons than the return of Robert Carewe why Rouen had lost the joy and mirth that belonged to it. Nay, the merry town had changed beyond all credence; it was hushed like a sick-room, and dolefully murmurous with forebodings of farewell and sorrow.

For all the very flower of Rouen's youth had promised to follow Tom Vanrevel on the long and arduous journey to Mexico, to march burning miles under the tropical sun, to face strange fevers and the guns of Santa Anna.

Few were the houses of the more pretentious sort that did not mourn, in prospect, the going of son, or brother, or close friend; mothers already wept not in secret, fathers talked with husky bravado; and everyone was very kind to those who were to go, speaking to them gently and bringing them little foolish presents. Nor could the hearts of girls now longer mask as blocks of ice to the prospective conquistadores; Eugene Madrillon's young brother, Jean, after a two years' Beatrice-and-Benedict wooing of Trixie Chenoweth (that notable spitfire) announced his engagement upon the day after his enlistment, and recounted to all who would listen how his termagant fell upon his neck in tears when she heard the news. "And now she cries about me all the time," finished the frank Jean blithely.

But there was little spirit for the old merriments: there were no more carpet-dances at the Bareauds', no masquerades at the Madrillons', no picnics in the woods nor excursions on the river; and no more did light feet bear light hearts through the "mazes of the intricate schottische, the subtle mazourka, or the stately quadrille," as Will Cummings remarked in the Journal. Fanchon, Virginia, and five or six others, spent their afternoons mournfully, and yet proudly, sewing and cutting large pieces of colored silk, fashioning a great flag for their sweethearts and brothers to bear southward and plant where stood the palace of the Montezumas.

That was sad work for Fanchon, though it was not for her brother's sake that she wept, since, as everyone knew, Jefferson was already so full of malaria and quinine that the fevers of the South and Mexico must find him invulnerable, and even his mother believed he would only thrive and grow hearty on his soldiering. But about Crailey, Fanchon had a presentiment more vivid than any born of the natural fears for his safety; it came to her again and again, reappearing in her dreams; she shivered and started often as she worked on the flag, then bent her fair head low over the gay silks, while the others glanced at her sympathetically. She had come to feel quite sure that Crailey was to be shot.

"But I've dreamed it—dreamed it six!" she cried, when he laughed, at her and tried to cheer her. "And it comes to me in the day-time as though I saw it with my eyes: the picture of you in an officer's uniform, lying on the fresh, green grass, and a red stain just below the throat."

"That shows what dreams are made of, dear lady," he smiled. "We'll find little green grass in Mexico, and I'm only a corporal; so where's the officer's uniform?"

Then Fanchon wept the more, and put her arms about him, while it seemed to her that she must cling to him so forever and thus withhold him from fulfilling her vision, and that the gentle pressure of her arms must somehow preserve him to life and to her. "Ah, you can't go, darling," she sobbed, while he petted her and tried to soothe her. "You can't leave me! You belong to me! They can't, can't, can't take you away from me!"

And when the flag was completed, save for sewing the stars upon the blue ground, she took it away from the others and insisted upon finishing the work herself. To her own room she carried it, and each of the white stars that the young men of Rouen were to follow in the struggle that would add so many others to the constellation, was jewelled with her tears and kissed by her lips as it took its place with its brothers. Never were neater stitches taken, for, with every atom of her body yearning to receive the shot that was destined for Crailey, this quiet sewing was all that she could do! She would have followed him, to hold a parasol over him under the dangerous sun, to cook his meals properly, to watch over him with medicines and blankets and a fan; she would have followed barefoot and bareheaded, and yet, her heart breaking with the crucial yearning to mother him and protect him, this was all that she could for him, this small stitching at the flag he had promised to follow.

When the work was quite finished, she went all over it again with double thread, not facing the superstition of her motive, which was to safeguard her lover: the bullet that was destined for Crailey might, in the myriad chances, strike the flag first and be deflected, though never so slightly, by one of these last stitches, and Crailey's heart thus missed by the same margin. It was at this juncture, when the weeping of women was plentiful, when old men pulled long faces, and the very urchins of the street observed periods of gravity and even silence, that a notion entered the head of Mrs. Tanberry—young Janie Tanberry—to the effect that such things were all wrong. She declared energetically that this was no decent fashion of farewell; that after the soldiers went away there would be time enough to enact the girls they had left behind them; and that, until then, the town should be made enlivening. So she went about preaching a revival of cheerfulness, waving her jewelled hand merrily from the Carewe carriage to the volunteers she saw upon the street, calling out to them with laughter and inspiring quip; everywhere scolding the mourners viciously in her husky voice, and leaving so much of heartening vivacity in her wake that none could fail to be convinced that she was a wise woman.

Nor was her vigor spent in vain. It was decided that a ball should be given to the volunteers of Rouen two nights before their departure for the State rendezvous, and it should be made the noblest festival in Rouen's history; the subscribers took their oath to it. They rented the big dining-room at the Rouen House, covered the floor with smooth cloth, and hung the walls solidly with banners and roses, for June had come. More, they ran a red carpet across the sidewalk (which was perfectly dry and clean) almost to the other side of the street; they imported two extra fiddles and a clarionet to enlarge the orchestra; and they commanded a supper such as a hungry man beholds in a dream.

Miss Betty laid out her prettiest dress that evening, and Mrs. Tanberry came in and worshipped it as it rested, like foam of lavender and white and gray, upon the bed, beside the snowy gloves with their tiny, stiff lace gauntlets, while two small white sandal-slippers, with jeweled buckles where the straps crossed each other, were being fastened upon Miss Betty's silken feet by the vain and gloating Mamie.

"It's a wicked cruelty, Princess!" exclaimed Mrs. Tanberry. "We want cheer the poor fellows and help them to be gay, and here do you deliberately plan to make them sick at the thought of leaving the place that holds you! Or have you discovered that there's one poor vagabond of the band getting off without having his heart broken, and made up your mind to do it for him tonight?"

"Is father to go with us?" asked Betty. It was through Mrs. Tanberry that she now derived all information concerning Mr. Carewe, as he had not directly addressed her since the afternoon when he discovered her reading the Journal's extra.

"No, we are to meet him' there. He seems rather pleasanter than usual this evening," remarked Mrs. Tanberry, hopefully, as she retired.

"Den we mus' git ready to share big trouble tomorrer!" commented the kneeling Mamie, with a giggle.

Alas! poor adoring servitress, she received a share unto herself that very evening, for her young mistress, usually as amiable as a fair summer sky, fidgetted, grumbled, found nothing well done, and was never two minutes in the same mind. After donning the selected dress, she declared it a fright, tried two others, abused each roundly, dismissed her almost weeping handmaiden abruptly, and again put on the first. Sitting down to the mirror, she spent a full hour over the arrangement of her hair, looking attentively at her image, sometimes with the beginning of doubtful approval, often angrily, and, now and then, beseechingly, imploring it to be lovely.

When Mrs. Tanberry came in to tell her that Nelson was at the block with the carriage, Miss Betty did not turn, and the elder lady stopped on the threshold and gave a quick, asthmatic gasp of delight. For the picture she saw was, without a doubt in the world, what she proclaimed it, a moment later, ravishingly pretty: the girlish little pink and white room with all its dainty settings for a background, lit by the dozen candles in their sconces and half as many slender silver candlesticks, and, seated before the twinkling mirror, the beautiful Miss Carewe, in her gown of lace and flounces that were crisp, yet soft, her rope of pearls, her white sandals, and all the glory of her youth. She had wound a wreath of white roses into her hair, her cheeks were flushed, and her eyes warm and glowing, yet inscrutable in their long gaze into the mirror.

"Oh," said Mrs. Tanberry, "you make me want to be a man! I'd pick you up and run to the North Pole, where no one could ever follow. And I can tell you that it hurts not to throw my arms round you and kiss you; but you're so exquisite I don't want to touch you!"

In answer, Miss Betty ran to her and kissed her rapturously on both cheeks. "Am I—after all?" she cried. "Am I? Is it? Will the roses do?" And without heeding her companion's staccatoes of approval she went rapidly to the open bureau, snatched up a double handful of ribbons and furbelows, and dashed out of the room in search of the disgraced Mamie. She found her seated on the kitchen door-step in lonely lamentation, and showered the gifts into her lap, while the vain one shrieked inimitably with pride in the sudden vision of her mistress and joy of the incredible possessions.

"Here, and here,and here!" said Miss Betty in a breath, hurling the fineries upon her. "I'm an evil-tongued shrew, Mamie, and these aren't to make up for the pain I gave you, but just to show that I'd like to if I knew how! Good-by!" And she was off like an April breeze.

"Dance wid the han'somdest," screamed Mamie, pursuing uproariously to see the last of her as she jumped into the carriage, "bow to de wittriest, an' kiss de one you love de bes'!"

"That will be you!" said Miss Betty to Mrs. Tanberry, and kissed the good lady again.

CHAPTER XVI

"THOSE ENDEARING YOUNG CHARMS"

It is a matter not of notoriety but of the happiest celebrity that Mrs. Tanberry danced that night, and not only that she danced, but that she waltzed. To the lot of Tappingham Marsh (whom she pronounced the most wheedlmg vagabond, next to Crailey Gray, of her acquaintance) it fell to persuade her; and, after a quadrille with the elder Chenoweth, she was with Tappingham. More extraordinary to relate, she danced down both her partner and music. Thereupon did Mr. Bareaud, stung with envy, dare emulation and essay a schottische with Miss Trixie Chenoweth, performing marvelously well for many delectable turns before he unfortunately fell down. It was a night when a sculptured god would have danced on his pedestal: June, but not over-warm, balm in the air and rose leaves on the breeze; and even Minerva's great heels might have marked the time that orchestra kept. Be sure they waltzed again to "Those Endearing Young Charms ":

"Oh, the heart that has truly loved never forgets, But as truly loves on to the close: as the sunflower turns on her god when he sets, The same look that she gave when he rose."

Three of the volunteers were resplendent in their regimentals:

Mr. Marsh (who had been elected captain of the new company to succeed Vanrevel), and Will Cummings and Jean Madrillon, the lieutenants. This glory was confined to the officers, who had ordered their uniforms at home, for the privates and non-commissioned officers were to receive theirs at the State rendezvous. However, although this gala adornment was limited to the three gentlemen mentioned, their appearance added "an indescribable air of splendor and pathos to the occasion," to quote Mr. Cummings once more. A fourth citizen of the town who might have seized upon this opportunity to display himself as a soldier neglected to take advantage of it and stole in quietly, toward the last, in his ordinary attire, leaving his major's uniform folded on a chair in his own room. The flag was to be presented to the volunteers at the close of the evening, and Tom came for that—so he claimed to his accusing soul.

He entered unobserved and made his way, keeping close to the wall, to where Mrs. Bareaud sat, taking a chair at her side; but Robert Carewe, glancing thither by chance, saw him, and changed countenance for an instant. Mr. Carewe composed his features swiftly, excused himself with elaborate courtesy from Miss Chenoweth, with whom he was talking, and crossed the room to a corner near his enemy. Presently, as the music ceased, the volunteers were bidden to come forward, whereupon Tom left Mrs. Bareaud and began to work his way down the room. Groups were forming and breaking up in the general movement of the crowd, and the dissolving of one brought him face to face with Elizabeth Carewe, who was moving slowly in the opposite direction, a small flock of suitors in her train.

The confrontation came so suddenly and so unexpectedly that, before either was aware, they looked squarely into each other's eyes, full and straight, and both stopped instantly as though transfixed, Miss Betty leaving a sentence forever half-complete. There was a fierce, short vocal sound from the crowd behind Vanrevel; but no one noticed Mr. Carewe; and then Tom bowed gravely, as in apology for blocking the way, and passed on.

Miss Betty began to talk again, much at random, with a vivacity too greatly exaggerated to be genuine, while the high color went from her cheeks and left her pale. Nothing could have enraged her more with herself than the consciousness, now suddenly strong within her, that the encounter had a perceptible effect upon her. What power had this man to make her manner strained and mechanical? What right had his eyes always to stir her as they did? It was not he for whom she had spent an hour over her hair; not he for whom she had driven her poor handmaiden away in tears: that was for one who had not come, one great in heart and goodness, one of a pure and. sacrificial life who deserved all she could give, and for whose sake she had honored herself in trying to look as pretty as she could. He had not come; and that hurt her a little, but she felt his generosity, believing that his motive was to spare her, since she could not speak to him in Mr Carewe's presence without open and public rupture with her father. Well, she was almost ready for that, seeing how little of a father hers was! Ah! that other should have come, if only to stand between her and this tall hypocrite whose dark glance had such strength to disturb her. What lies that gaze contained, all in the one flash!—the strange pretence of comprehending her gently but completely, a sad compassion, too, and with it a look of farewell, seeming to say: "Once more I have come for this—and just, 'Good-by!'" For she knew that he was going with the others, going perhaps forever, only the day after tomorrow—then she would see him no more and be free of him. Let the day after tomorrow come soon! Miss Betty hated herself for understanding the adieu, and hated herself more because she could not be sure that, in the startled moment of meeting before she collected herself, she had let it go unanswered.

She had done more than that: without knowing it she had bent her head to his bow, and Mr. Carewe had seen both the salutation and the look.

The young men were gathered near the orchestra, and, to the hilarious strains of "Yankee Doodle," the flag they were to receive for their regiment was borne down the room by the sisters and sweethearts who had made it, all of whom were there, except Fanchon Bareaud. Crailey had persuaded her to surrender the flag for the sake of spending this evening - next to his last in Rouen—at home alone with him.

The elder Chenoweth made the speech of presentation, that is, he made part of it before he broke down, for his son stood in the ranks of the devoted band. Until this incident occurred, all had gone trippingly, for everyone had tried to put the day after to-morrow from his mind. Perhaps there might not have been so many tears even now, if the young men had not stood together so smilingly to receive their gift; it was seeing them so gay and confident, so strong in their youth and so unselfish of purpose; it was this, and the feeling that all of them must suffer and some of them die before they came back. So that when Mr. Chenoweth, choking in his loftiest flight, came to a full stop, and without disguise buried his face in his handkerchief, Mrs. Tanberry, the apostle of gayety, openly sobbed. Chenoweth, without more ado, carried the flag over to Tappingham Marsh, whom Vanrevel directed to receive it, and Tappingham thanked the donors without many words, because there were not then many at his command.

Miss Carewe bad been chosen to sing "The Star Spangled Banner," and she stepped out a little from the crowd to face the young men as the orchestra sounded the first chord. She sang in a full, clear voice, but when the volunteers saw that, as she sang, the tears were streaming down her cheeks in spite of the brave voice, they began to choke with the others. If Miss Betty found them worth weeping for, they could afford to cry a little for themselves. Yet they joined the chorus nobly, and raised the roof with the ringing song, sending the flamboyant, proud old words thunderously to heaven.

That was not the last song of the night. General Trumble and Mr. Chenoweth had invited their young friends to attend, after the ball, a collation which they chose to call a supper, but which, to accord with the hour, might more aptly have been designated a breakfast. To afford a private retreat for the scene of this celebration, they had borrowed the offices of Gray and Vanrevel, and Crailey hospitably announced that any guest was welcome to stay for a year or two, since, probably, neither of the firm would have need of an office for at least that length of time. Nine men gathered about the table which replaced Tom's work-a-day old desk: the two Chenoweths, Eugene Madrillon, Marsh, Jefferson Bareaud, the stout General, Tom Vanrevel, Crailey, and Will Cummings, the editor coming in a little late, but rubbing his hands cheerfully over what he declared was to be the last column from his pen to rear its length on the Journal's front page for many a long day—a description of the presentation of the flag, a bit of prose which he considered almost equal to his report of the warehouse fire.

This convivial party made merry and tried to forget that most of them had "been mighty teary," as Marsh said, an hour earlier; while Mr. Chenoweth sat with his hand on his son's shoulder, unconsciously most of the time, apologetically removing, it when he observed it. Many were the witticisms concerning the difference in rank hence forth to be observed between the young men, as Tom was now a major, Marsh a captain, Will Cummings a second lieutenant, and the rest mere privates, except Crailey, who was a corporal. Nevertheless, though the board was festive, it was somewhat subdued and absent until they came to the toasts.

It was Tappingham who proposed Miss Betty Carewe. "I know Tom Vanrevel will understand—nay, I know he's man enough to join us," said Marsh as he rose. "Why shouldn't I say that we may hail ourselves as patriots, indeed, since at the call of our country we depart from the town which is this lady's home, and at the trumpet's sound resign the gracious blessing of seeing her day by day, and why shouldn't we admit loyally and openly that it is her image alone which shines in the hearts of most of us here?"

And no man arose to contradict that speech, which appears to have rung true, seeing that four of those present had proposed to her (again) that same evening. "So I give you," cried Tappingham, gallantly, "the health of Miss Betty Carewe, the loveliest rose of our bouquet! May she remember us when we come home!"

They rose and drank it with a shout. But Tom Vanrevel, not setting down his cup, went to the window and threw wide the shutters, letting in a ruddy shaft of the morning sun, so that as he stood in the strong glow he looked like a man carved out of red gold. He lifted his glass, not toward the table and his companions, while they stared at him, surprised, but toward the locusts of Carewe Street.

"To Miss Betty Carewe," he said, "the finest flower of them all! May she remember those who never come home!"

And, without pausing, he lifted his rich baritone in an old song that had been vastly popular with the young men of Rouen ever since the night of Miss Betty's debut; they had hummed it as they went about their daily work, they had whistled it on the streets; they had drifted, into dreams at night with the sound of it still chiming in their ears; and now, with one accord, as they stood gathered together for the last time in Rouen, they joined Tom Vanrevel and sang it again. And the eyes of Crailey Gray rested very gently upon his best friend as they sang:

"Believe me, If all those endearing young charms, Which I gaze on so fondly to-day, Were to change by to-morrow and fleet from my arms, Like fairy gifts fading away, Thou wouldst still be adored as this moment thou art: Let thy loveliness fade as it will, And around the dear ruin, each wish of my heart Would entwine itself verdantly still."

CHAPTER XVII

THE PRICE OF SILENCE

It was the misfortune of Mr. Cummings's first literary offering to annoy one of the editor's friends. The Journal was brought to the corporal at noon, while he was considering whether he should rise from his couch or sleep another hour. Reclining among his pillows, he glanced through Cummings's description with the subdued giggle he always had for the good William's style but as his eye fell upon one paragraph he started sat upright, and proceeded to read the passage several times with anxious attention.

"Only two or three sources of regret occurred to mar the delight (in which young and old participated) of that festal and dazzling scene. One was the absence of Miss Fanchon Bareaud, one the donors; another, that of Corporal Gray; a third was the excessive modesty of Major Vanrevel, although present at the time, refused to receive the ladies' sumptuous offering and insisted that Captain Marsh was the proper person to do the honors, to which the latter reluctantly, though gracefully consented. Also, we were sorry that the Major appeared in citizen's dress, as all were anxious to witness him in his uniform. However, in our humble judgment, he will be compelled by etiquette to don it this afternoon, to receive the officers of the regular army, who will arrive by the stage about five o'clock, it is expected, to inspect the company and swear them into the service of the Federal Government at the Court House. We, for one, have little doubt that, owing to the Major's well-known talent in matters of apparel, his appearance will far eclipse in brilliancy that of his fellow-officers."

Crailey dressed slowly, returning to the paper, now and then, with a perturbed countenance. How would Miss Betty explain this paragraph to herself, and how account for the fact that she had not seen Crailey, how for the fact that she had seen Tom? It seemed unlikely that she could have overlooked the latter—Tom was one of those whom everybody saw, wherever he went. And what inquiries would she make? For Crailey had no means of knowing that she would not see the Journal. Tomorrow he would be gone, it would be all over, but he wanted this last day to run smoothly. What wild hopes he had of things that should happen when they all came marching home, no one can say; even if it were not to be doubted that Crailey ever entertained hopes of any kind whatever, since to hope is to bestow thought upon the future.

But, however affairs ran with him so far as hope was concerned, he seldom lacked an idea; and one came to him presently, a notion that put the frown to rout and brought the old smile to his lips, his smile of the world-worn and tolerant prelate. He flicked the paper lightly from him, and it sped across the room like a big bird in awkward flight. For he knew how to preserve his last day as he wished, and to make all smooth.

He finished his toilet with particular care, took a flower from a vase on his table, placed it in his coat, and went down to the dusty street, where everything was warm and bright with summer. It was joy to be alive; there was wine enough in the air; and Crailey made up his mind not to take a drink that day—the last day! The last day! The three words kept ringing through his head like a minor phrase from a song. Tomorrow, at noon, they would be churning down the river; and this was the last day—the last day!

"Still not too late to make another friend at home," he said, stopping to pat the head of a mangy street cur that came crouching and wobbling toward him like a staveless little keg worried by scurries of wind. Dogs and children always fell in love with Crailey at first sight, and he never failed to receive them in the spirit of their approach. Now the mongrel, at his touch, immediately turned himself over and lay upon the pavement with all paws in air, to say: "Great lord, magnificent in the graciousness which deigns to cast a glimpse upon this abject cluster of ribs, I perceive that your heart is too gentle to kick me in my present helplessness; yet do with me as you will."

"I doubt if you've breakfasted, brother," Crailey responded aloud, rubbing the dog's head softly with the tip of his boot. "Will you share the meagre fare of one who is a poet, should be a lawyer, but is about to become a soldier? Eh, but a corporal! Rise, my friend. Up! and be in your own small self a whole Corporal's Guard! And if your Corporal doesn't come home from the wars, perhaps you'll remember him kindly? Think?"

He made a vivacious gesture, the small animal sprang into the air, convoluted with gratitude and new love, while Crailey, laughing softly, led the way to the hotel. There, while he ate sparsely himself, he provided munificently for his new acquaintance, and recommended him, with an accompaniment of silver, to the good offices of the Rouen House kitchen. After that, out into the sunshine again he went, with elastic step, and a merry word and a laugh for everyone he met. At the old English gardener's he bought four or five bouquets, and carried them on a round of visits of farewell to as many old ladies who had been kind to him. This done, leaving his laughter and his flowers behind him, he went to Fanchon and spent part of the afternoon bringing forth cunning arguments cheerily, to prove to her that General Taylor would be in the Mexican capital before the volunteers reached New Orleans, and urging upon her his belief that they would all be back in Rouen before the summer was gone.

But Fanchon could only sob and whisper, "Hush, hush!" in the dim room where they sat, the windows darkened so that, after he had gone, he should not remember how red her eyes were, and the purple depths under them, and thus forget how pretty she had been at her best. After a time, finding that the more he tried to cheer her, the more brokenly she wept, he grew silent, only stroking her head, while the summer sounds came in through the window: the mill-whir of locusts, the small monotone of distant farm-bells, the laughter of children in the street, and the gay arias of a mocking-bird singing in the open window of the next house. So they sat together through the long, still afternoon of the last day.

No one in Rouen found that afternoon particularly enlivening. Even Mrs. Tanberry gave way to the common depression, and, once more, her doctrine of cheerfulness relegated to the ghostly ranks of the purely theoretical, she bowed under the burden of her woe so far as to sing "Methought I Met a Damsel Fair" (her of the bursting sighs) at the piano. Whenever sadness lay upon her soul she had acquired the habit of resorting to this unhappy ballad; today she sang it four times. Mr. Carewe was not at home, and had announced that though he intended to honor the evening meal by his attendance, he should be away for the evening itself; as comment upon which statement Mrs. Tanberry had offered ambiguously the one word, "Amen!" He was stung to no reply, and she had noted the circumstance as unusual, and also that he had appeared to labor with the suppression of a keen excitement, which made him anxious to escape from her sharp little eyes; an agitation for which she easily accounted when she recalled that he had seen Vanrevel on the previous evening. Mr. Carewe had kept his promise to preserve the peace, as he always kept it when the two met on neutral ground, but she had observed that his face showed a kind of hard-leashed violence whenever he had been forced to breathe the air of the same room with his enemy, and that the thing grew on him.

Miss Betty exhibited not precisely a burning interest in the adventure of the Damsel Fair, wandering out of the room during the second rendition, wandering back again, and once more away. She had moved about the house in this fashion since early morning, wearing what Mamie described as a "peak-ed look." White-faced and restless, with distressed eyes, to which no sleep had come in the night, she could not read; she could no more than touch her harp; she could not sleep; she could not remain quiet for three minutes together. Often she sank into a chair with an air of languor and weariness, only to start immediately out of it and seek some other part of the house, or to go and pace the garden. Here, in the air heavy with roses and tremulous with June, as she walked rapidly up and down, late in the afternoon, at the time when the faraway farm-bells were calling men from the fields to supper, the climax of her restlessness came. That anguish and desperation, so old in her sex, the rebellion against the law that inaction must be her part, had fallen upon her for the first time. She came to an abrupt stop and struck her hands together despairingly, and spoke aloud.

"What shall I do! What shall I do!"

"Ma'am?" asked a surprised voice, just behind her.

She wheeled quickly about, to behold a shock-headed urchin of ten in the path near the little clearing. He was ragged, tanned, dusty, neither shoes nor coat trammelling his independence; and be had evidently entered the garden through the gap in the hedge.

"I thought you spoke to me?" he said, inquiringly.

"I didn't see you," she returned. "What is it?"

"You Miss Carewe?" he asked; but before she could answer he said, reassuringly, "Why, of course you are! I remember you perfect, now I git the light on you, so to speak. Don't you remember me?"

"No, I don't think I do."

"Lord!" he responded, wonderingly. "I was one of the boys with you on them boxes the night of your pa's fire!" Mingled with the surprise in his tone was a respectful unction which intimated how greatly he honored her father for having been the owner of so satisfactory a conflagration.

"Were you? Perhaps I'll remember you if you give me time."

But at this point the youth recalled the fact that he had an errand to discharge, and, assuming an expression of businesslike haste too pressing to permit farther parley, sought in his pocket and produced a sealed envelope, with which he advanced upon her.

"Here. There's an answer. He told me not to tell nobody who sent it, and not to give it to nobody on earth but you, and how to slip in through the hedge and try and find you in the garden when nobody was lookin', and he give a pencil for you to answer on the back of it, and a dollar."

Miss Betty took the note, glancing once over her shoulder at the house, but Mrs. Tanberry was still occupied with the Maiden, and no one was in sight. She read the message hastily.

"I have obeyed you, and shall always. You have not sent for me. Perhaps that was because there was no time when you thought it safe. Perhaps you have still felt there would be a loss of dignity. Does that weigh with you against good-by? Tell me, if you can, that you have it in your heart to let me go without seeing you once more, without good-by—for the last time. Or was it untrue that you wrote me what you did? Was that dear letter but a little fairy dream of mine? Ah, will you see me again, this once—this once—let me look at you, let me talk with you, hear your voice? The last time!"

There was no signature.

Miss Betty quickly wrote four lines upon the same sheet: "Yes—yes! I must see you, must talk with you before you go. Come at dusk. The garden—near the gap in the hedge. It will be safe for a little while. He will not be here." She replaced the paper in its envelope, drew a line through her own name on the letter, and wrote "Mr. Vanrevel" underneath.

"Do you know the gentleman who sent you? "she asked.

"No'm; but he'll be waitin' at his office, 'Gray and Vanrevel,' on Main Street, for the answer."

"Then hurry!" said Betty.

He needed no second bidding, but, with wings on his bare

heels, made off through the gap in the hedge. At the corner of the street he encountered an adventure, a gentleman's legs and a heavy hand at the same time. The hand fell on his shoulder, arresting his scamper with a vicious jerk; and the boy was too awed to attempt an escape, for he knew his captor well by sight, although never before had he found himself so directly in the company of Rouen's richest citizen. The note dropped from the small trembling fingers, yet those fingers did not shake as did the man's when, like a flash, Carewe seized upon the missive with his disengaged hand and saw what two names were on the envelope.

"You were stealing, were you! " he cried, savagely. "I saw you sneak through my hedge!"

"I didn't, either!"

Mr. Carewe ground his teeth, "What were you doing there?"

"Nothing!"

"Nothing!" mocked Carewe. "Nothing!

You didn't carry this to the young lady in there and get her answer?"

"No, sir!" answered the captive, earnestly.

"Cross my heart I didn't. I found it!"

Slowly the corrugations of anger were levelled from the magnate's face, the white heat cooled, and the prisoner marvelled to find himself in the presence of an urbane gentleman whose placidity made the scene of a moment ago appear some trick of distorted vision. And yet, curious to behold, Mr. Carewe's fingers shook even more violently than before, as he released the boy's shoulder and gave him a friendly tap on the head, at the same time smiling benevolently.

"There, there," he said, bestowing a wink upon the youngster. "It's all right; it doesn't matter—only I think I see the chance of a jest in this. You wait, while I read this little note, this message that you found!" He ended by winking again with the friendliest drollery.

He turned his back to the boy, and opened the note; continuing to stand in that position while he read the two messages. It struck the messenger that, after this, there need be no great shame in his own lack of this much-vaunted art of reading, since it took so famous a man as Mr. Carewe such length of time to peruse a little note. But perhaps the great gentleman was ill, for it appeared to the boy that he lurched several times, once so far that he would have gone over if he had not saved himself by a lucky stagger. And once, except for the fact that the face that had turned away had worn an expression of such genial humor, the boy would have believed that from it issued a sound like the gnashing of teeth.

But when it was turned to him again, it bore the same amiable jocosity of mouth and eye, and nothing seemed to be the matter, except that those fingers still shook so wildly, too wildly, indeed, to restore the note to its envelope.

"There," said Mr. Carewe, "put it back, laddie, put it back yourself. Take it to the gentleman who sent you. I see he's even disguised his hand a trifle-ha! ha!—and I suppose he may not have expected the young lady to write his name quite so boldly on the envelope! What do you suppose?"

"I d'know," returned the boy. "I reckon I don't hardly understand."

"No, of course not," said Mr. Carewe, laughing rather madly. "Ha, ha, ha! Of course you wouldn't. And how much did he give you?"

"Yay!" cried the other, joyously. "Didn't he go and hand me a dollar!"

"How much will you take not to tell him that I stopped you and read it; how much not to speak of me at all?"

"What?"

"It's a foolish kind of joke, nothing more. I'll give you five dollars never to tell anyone that you saw me today."

"Don't shoot, Colonel," exclaimed the youth, with a riotous fling of bare feet in the air, "I'll come down!"

"You'll do it?"

"Five!" he shouted, dancing upon the boards. "Five! I'll cross my heart to die I never hear tell of you, or ever knew they was sich a man in the world!"

Carewe bent over him. "No! Say: 'God strike me dead and condemn me eternally to the everlasting flames of hell if I ever tell!'"

This entailed quick sobriety, though only benevolence was in the face above him. The jig-step stopped, and the boy pondered, frightened.

"Have I got to say that?"

Mr. Carewe produced a bank-bill about which the boy beheld a halo. Clearly this was his day; heaven showed its approval of his conduct by an outpouring of imperishable riches. And yet the oath misliked him; there was a savor of the demoniacal contract; still that was to be borne and the plunge taken, for there fluttered the huge sum before his dazzled eyes. He took a deep breath. "'God strike me dead' "—he began, slowly—"' if I ever '—"

"No. 'And condemn me to the everlasting flames of hell '—"

"Have I got to?"

"Yes."

—" 'And condemn me to—to the everlasting flames of—of hell, if I ever tell!'"

He ran off, pale with the fear that he might grow up, take to drink and some day tell in his cups, but so resolved not to coquet with temptation that he went round a block to avoid the door of the Rouen House bar. Nevertheless, the note was in his hand and the fortune in his pocket

And Mr. Carewe was safe. He knew that the boy would never tell, and he knew another thing, for he had read the Journal, though it came no more to his house: he knew that Tom Vanrevel wore his uniform that evening, and that, even in the dusk, the brass buttons on an officer's breast make a good mark for a gun steadied along the ledge of a window. As he entered the gates and went toward the house he glanced up at the window which overlooked his garden from the cupola.

CHAPTER XVIII

THE UNIFORM

Crailey was not the only man in Rouen who had been saying to himself all day that each accustomed thing he did was done for the last time. Many of his comrades went about with "Farewell, old friend," in their hearts, not only for the people, but for the usual things of life and the actions of habit, now become unexpectedly dear and sweet to know or to perform. So Tom Vanrevel, relieved of his hot uniform, loose as to collar, wearing a big dressing-gown, and stretched in a chair, watched the sunset from the western window of the dusty office, where he had dreamed through many sunsets in summers past, and now took his leave of this old habit of his in silence, with a long cigar, considering the chances largely against his ever seeing the sun go down behind the long wooden bridge at the foot of Main Street again.

The ruins of the warehouses had been removed, and the river was laid clear to his sight; it ran between brown banks like a river of rubies, and, at the wharf, the small evening steamboat, ugly and grim enough to behold from near by, lay pink and lovely in that broad glow, tooting imminent departure, although an hour might elapse before it would back into the current. The sun widened, clung briefly to the horizon, and dropped behind the low hills beyond the bottom lands; the stream grew purple, then took on a lustre of pearl as the stars came out, while rosy distances changed to misty blue; the chatter of the birds in the Main Street maples became quieter, and, through lessening little choruses of twittering, fell gradually to silence. And now the blue dusk crept on the town, and the corner drug-store window-lights threw mottled colors on the pavement. >From the hall, outside the closed office-door, came the sound of quick, light footsteps; it was Crailey going out; but Tom only sighed to himself, and did not hail him. So these light footsteps of Crailey Gray echoed but a moment in the stairway and were heard no more.

A few moments later a tall figure, dressed from neck to heels in a gray cloak crossed the mottled lights, and disappeared into Carewe Street. This cloaked person wore on his head a soldier's cap, and Tom, not recognizing him surely, vaguely wondered why Tappingham Marsh chose to muffle himself so warmly on a evening. He noted the quick, alert tread as like Marsh's usual gait, but no suspicion crossed his mind that the figure might be that of partner.

A rocket went up from the Rouen House, then another, followed by a salvo of anvils and rackety discharge of small-arms; the beginning a noble display of fireworks in celebration of prospective victories of the United States and utter discomfiture of the Mexicans when the Rouen Volunteers should reach the seat of war, an Exhibition of patriotism which brought little pleasure to Mr. Vanrevel.

But over the noise of the street he heard his own name shouted from the stairway, and almost instantly a violent knocking assailed the door. Before he could bid the visitor enter, the door was flung open by a stout and excited colored woman, who, at sight of him, threw up her hands in tremulous thanksgiving. It was the vain Mamie.

She sank into a chair, and rocked herself to and fro, gasping to regain her lost breath. "Bless de good God 'Imighty you am' gone out!" she panted. "I run an' I run, an' I come so fas' I got stitches in de side f'um head to heel!"

Tom brought her a glass of water, which she drank between gasps.

"I nevah run so befo' enduin' my livin' days," she asserted. "You knows me, who I am an' whum I cum f'um, nigh's well's I knows who you is, I reckon, Maje' Vanrevel?"

"Yes, yes, I know. Will you tell me who sent you?"

"Miz Tanberry, suh, dat who sended me, an' in a venomous hurry she done de same!"

"Yes. Why? Does she want me?"

Mamie emitted a screech. "'Deed she mos' everlas'in'ly does not! Dat de ve'y exackindes' livin' t'ing she does not want!"

"Then what is it, Mamie?"

"Lemme git my bref, suh, an' you hole yo'ne whiles I tell you! She say to me, she say: 'Is you 'quainted Maje' Vanrevel, Mamie?' s' she, an' I up'n' ansuh, 'Not to speak wid, but dey ain; none on 'em I don' knows by sight, an' none betterer dan him,' I say. Den she say, she say: 'You run all de way an' fin' dat young man,' she say, s' she, 'an' if you don' git dah fo' he leave, er don' stop him on de way, den God 'imighty fergive you!' she say. 'But you tell him f'um Jane Tanberry not to come nigh dis house or dis gyahden dis night! Tell him dat Jane Tanberry warn him he mus' keep outer Carewe's way ontel he safe on de boat to-morrer. Tell him Jane Tanberry beg him to stay in he own room dis night, an' dat she beg it on her bented knees!' An' dis she say to me when I tole her what Nelson see in dat house dis evenin'. An' hyuh I is, an' hyuh yew is, an' de blessed Jesus be thank', you ir hyuh!"

Tom regarded her with a grave attention. "What made Mrs. Tanberry think I might be coming there to-night?"

"Dey's cur'ous goin's-on in dat house, suh! De young lady she ain' like herself; all de day long she wanduh up an' down an' roun' about. Miz Tanberry are a mighty guessifying woman, an' de minute I tell her what Nelse see, she s'pec' you a-comin' an' dat de boss mos' pintedly preparin' fo' it!"

"Can you make it a little clearer for me, Mamie? I'm afraid I don't understand."

"Well, suh, you know dat ole man Nelson, he allays tell me ev'yt'ing he know, an' ev'yt'ing he think he know, jass de same, suh. An' dat ole Nelse, he mos' 'sessful cull'd man in de worl' to crope roun' de house an' pick up de gossip an' git de 'fo' an' behine er what's goin' on. So 'twas dat he see de boss, when he come in to'des evenin', tek dat heavy musket offn' de racks an' load an' clean her, an' he do it wid a mighty bad look 'bout de mouf. Den he gone up to de cupoly an' lef' it dah, an' den come down ag'in. Whiles dey all is eatin', he 'nounce th'ee time' dat he goin' be 'way endu'in' de evenin'. Den he gone out de front do', an' out de gates, an' down de street. Den, su, den, suh, 'tain't no mo'n a half-'n-'our ago, Nelse come to me an' say dat he see de boss come roun' de stable, keepin' close in by de shrubbery, an' crope in de ball-room winder, w'ich is close to de groun', suh. Nelse 'uz a cleanin' de harness in de back yo'd an' he let on not to see him, like. Miss Betty, she walkin' in her gyahden an' Miz Tanberry fan' on de po'ch. Nelse, he slip de house whuh de lights ain' lit, an' stan' an' listen long time in de liberry at de foot er dem sta'hs; an' he hyuh dat man move, suh! Den Nelse know dat he done crope up to de cupoly room an'—an' dat he settin' dah, waitin'! Soze he come an' tole me, an' I beg Miz Tanberry come in de kitchen, an' I shet de do' an' I tole her. An' she sended me hyuh to you, suh. An' if you 'uz a-goin', de good God 'lmighty mus' er kep' you ontel I got hyuh!"

"No; I wasn't going." Tom smiled upon her sadly. "I dare say there's a simpler explanation. Don't you suppose that if Nelson was right and Mr. Carewe really did come back, it was because he did not wish his daughter and Mrs. Tanberry to know that—that he expected a party of friends, possibly, to join him there later?"

"What he doin' wid dat gun, suh? Nobody goin' play cyahds ner frow dice wid a gun, is dey?" asked Mamie, as she rose and walked toward the door.

"Oh, that was probably by chance."

"No, suh!" she cried, vehemently. "An' dem gelmun wouldn' play t'-night, no way; mos' on 'em goin' wid you to-morrer an' dey sayin' goodby to de'r folks dis evenin', not gamblin'! Miz Tanberry'll be in a state er mine ontel she hyuh f'um me, an' I goin' hurry back. You won' come dah, suh? I kin tell her dat you say you sutney ain' comin' nigh our neighborhood dis night?"

"I had not dreamed of coming, tell her, please. Probably I shall not go out at all this evening. But it was kind of you to come. Good-night."

He stood with a candle to light her down the stairs, but after she had gone he did not return to the office. Instead, he went slowly up to his own room, glancing first into Crailey's—the doors of neither were often locked—to behold a chaos of disorder and unfinished packing. In his own chamber it only remained for him to close the lids of a few big boxes, and to pack a small trunk which he meant to take with him to the camp of the State troops, and he would be ready for departure. He set about this task, arid, concluding that there was no necessity to wear his uniform on the steamboat, decided to place it in the trunk, and went to the bed where he had folded and left it. It was not there. Nor did a thorough search reveal it anywhere in the room. Yet no one could have stolen it, for when he had gone down to the office Crailey had remained on this floor. Mamie had come within a few minutes after Crailey went out, and during his conversation with her the office-door had been open; no one could have passed without being seen. Also, a thief would have taken other things as well as the uniform; and surely Crailey must have heard; Crailey would—Crailey—!

Then Tom remembered the figure in the long cloak and the military cap, and, with a sick heart, began to understand. He had read the Journal, and he knew why Crailey might wish to masquerade in a major's uniform that night. If Miss Carewe read it too, and a strange wonder rose in her mind, this and a word would convince her. Tom considered it improbable that the wonder would rise, for circumstances had too well established her in a mistake, trivial and ordinary enough at first, merely the confusing of two names by a girl new to the town, but so strengthened by every confirmation Crailey's wit could compass that she would, no doubt, only set Cummings's paragraph aside as a newspaper error. Still, Crailey had wished to be on the safe side!

Tom sighed rather bitterly. He was convinced that the harlequin would come home soon, replace the uniform (which was probably extremely becoming to him, as they were of a height and figure much the same), and afterward, in his ordinary dress, would sally forth to spend his last evening with Fanchon. Tom wondered how Crailey would feel and what he would think about himself while he was changing his clothes, but he remembered his partner's extraordinary powers of mental adjustment—and for the first time in his life Vanrevel made no allowance for the other's temperament, and there came to him a moment when he felt that he could almost dislike Crailey Gray

At all events, he would go out until Crailey had come and left again, for he had no desire to behold the masquerader's return. So he exchanged his dressing-gown for a coat, fastened his collar, and had begun to arrange his cravat at the mirror, when, suddenly, the voice of the old negress seemed to sound close beside him in the room

"He's settin' dah—waitin'!"

The cravat was never tied; Tom's hands dropped , to his sides as he started back from the staring face in the mirror. Robert Carewe was waiting—and Crailey—All at once there was but one vital necessity in the world for Tom Vanrevel, that was to find Crailey; he must go to Crailey—even in Carewe's own house—he must go to Crailey!

He dashed down the stairs and into the street. The people were making a great uproar in front of the hotel, exploding bombs, firing muskets in the air, sending up rockets; and rapidly crossing the outskirts of the crowd, he passed into Carewe Street, unnoticed. Here the detonations were not so deafening, though the little steamboat at the wharf was contributing to the confusion with all in her power, screeching simultaneously approval of the celebration and her last signals of departure.

At the first corner Tom had no more than left the sidewalk

when he came within a foot of being ridden down by two horsemen who rode at so desperate a gallop that (the sound of their hoof-beats being lost in the uproar from Main Street) they were upon him before he was aware of them.

He leaped back with an angry shout to know who they were that they rode so wildly. At the same time a sharp explosion at the foot of the street sent a red flare over the scene, a flash, gone with such incredible swiftness into renewed darkness that he saw the flying horsemen almost as equestrian statues illumined by a flicker of lightning, but he saw them with the same distinctness that lightning gives, and recognized the foremost as Robert Carewe. And in the instant of that recognition, Tom knew what had happened to Crailey Gray, for he saw the truth in the ghastly face of his enemy.

Carewe rode stiffly, like a man frozen upon his horse, and his face was like that of a frozen man; his eyes glassy and not fixed upon his course, so that it was a deathly thing to see. Once, long ago, Tom had seen a man riding for his life, and he wore this same look. The animal bounded and swerved under Vanrevel's enemy in the mad rush down the street, but he sat rigid, bolt upright in the saddle, his face set to that look of coldness.

The second rider was old Nelson, who rode with body crouched forward, his eyeballs like shining porcelain set in ebony, and his arm like a flail, cruelly lashing his own horse and his master's with a heavy whip. "De steamboat!" be shouted, hoarsely, bringing down the lash on one and then on the other. "De steamboat, de steamboat—f o' God's sake, honey, de steamboat!"

They swept into Main Street, Nelson leaning far across to the other's bridle, and turning both horses toward the river, but before they had made the corner, Tom Vanrevel was running with all the speed that was in him toward his enemy's house. The one block between him and that forbidden ground seemed to him miles long, and he felt that he was running as a man in a dream, and, at the highest pitch of agonized exertion, covering no space, but only working the air in one place, like a treadmill. All that was in his mind, heart, and soul was to reach Crailey. He had known by the revelation of Carewe's face in what case he would find his friend; but as he ran he put the knowledge from him with a great shudder, and resolved upon incredulity in spite of his certainty. All he let himself feel was the need to run, to run until he found Crailey, who was somewhere in the darkness of the trees about the long, low house on the corner. When he reached the bordering hedge, he did not stay for gate or path, but, with a loud shout, hurled himself half over, half through, the hedge, like a bolt from a catapult.

Lights shone from only one room in the house, the library; but as he ran toward the porch a candle flickered in the hall, and there came the sound of a voice weeping with terror.

At that he called more desperately upon his incredulity to aid him, for the voice was Mrs. Tan-berry's. If it had been any other than she, who sobbed so hopelessly—she who was always steady and strong! If he could, he would have stopped to pray, now, before he faced her and the truth; but his flying feet carried him on.

"Who is it?" she gasped, brokenly, from the hall. "Mamie? Have you brought him?"

"It's I," he cried, as he plunged through the doorway. "It's Vanrevel."

Mrs. Tanberry set the iron candlestick down upon the table with a crash.

"You've come too late!" she sobbed. "Another man has taken your death on himself."

He reeled back against the wall. "Oh, God!" he said. "Oh, God, God, God! Crailey!"

"Yes," she answered. "It's the poor vagabond that you loved so well."

Together they ran through the hall to the library. Crailey was lying on the long sofa, his eyes closed, his head like a piece of carven marble, the gay uniform, in which he had tricked himself out so gallantly, open at the throat, and his white linen stained with a few little splotches of red.

Beside him knelt Miss Betty, holding her lace handkerchief upon his breast; she was as white as he, and as motionless; so that, as she knelt there, immovable beside him, her arm like alabaster across his breast, they might have been a sculptor's group. The handkerchief was stained a little, like the linen, and like it, too, stained but a little. Nearby, on the floor, stood a flask of brandy and a pitcher of water.

"You!" Miss Betty's face showed no change, nor even a faint surprise, as her eyes fell upon Tom Vanrevel, but her lips soundlessly framed the word. "You!"

Tom flung himself on his knees beside her.

"Crailey!" he cried, in a sharp voice that had a terrible shake in it. "Crailey! Crailey, I want you to hear me!" He took one of the limp hands in his and began to chafe it, while Mrs. Tanberry grasped the other.

"There's still a movement in the pulse," she faltered.

"Still!" echoed Tom, roughly. "You're mad! You made me think Crailey was dead! Do you think Crailey Gray is going to die? He couldn't, I tell you—he couldn't; you don't know him! Who's gone for the doctor?" He dashed some brandy upon his handkerchief and set it to the white lips.

"Mamie. She was here in the room with me when it happened."

"'Happened'! 'Happened'!" he mocked her, furiously. "'Happened' is a beautiful word!"

"God forgive me!" sobbed Mrs. Tanberry. " I was sitting in the library, and Mamie had just come from you, when we heard Mr. Carewe shout from the cupola room: 'Stand away from my daughter, Vanrevel, and take this like a dog!' Only that;—and Mamie and I ran to the window, and we saw through the dusk a man in uniform leap back from Miss Betty—they were in that little open space near the hedge. He called out something and waved his hand, but the shot came at the same time, and he fell. Even then I was sure, in spite of what Mamie had said, I was as sure as Robert Carewe was, that it was you. He came and took one look—and saw—and then Nelson brought the horses and made him mount and go. Mamie ran for the doctor, and Betty and I carried Crailey in. It was hard work."

Miss Betty's hand had fallen from Crailey's breast where Tom's took its place. She rose unsteadily to her feet and pushed back the hair from her forehead, shivering convulsively as she looked down at the motionless figure on the sofa.

"Crailey!" said Tom, in the same angry, shaking voice. "Crailey, you've got to rouse yourself! This won't do; you've got to be a man! Crailey!" He was trying to force the brandy through the tightly clenched teeth. " Crailey! "

"Crailey!" whispered Miss Betty, leaning. heavily on the back of a chair. "Crailey?" She looked at Mrs. Tanberry with vague interrogation, but Mrs. Tanberry did not understand.

"Crailey!"

It was then that Crailey's eyelids fluttered and slowly opened; and his wandering glance, dull at first, slowly grew clear and twinkling as it rested on the ashy, stricken face of his best friend.

"Tom," he said, feebly, "it was worth the price, to wear your clothes just once!"

And then, at last, Miss Betty saw and understood. For not the honest gentleman, whom everyone except Robert Carewe held in esteem and affection, not her father's enemy, Vanrevel, lay before her with the death-wound in his breast for her sake, but that other—Crailey Gray, the ne'er-do-weel and light-o'-love, Crailey Gray, wit, poet, and scapegrace, the well-beloved town scamp.

He saw that she knew, and, as his brightening eyes wandered up to her, he smiled faintly. "Even a bad dog likes to have his day," he whispered.

CHAPTER XIX

THE FLAG GOES MARCHING BY

Will Cummings had abandoned the pen for the sword until such time as Santa Anna should cry for quarter, and had left the office in charge of an imported substitute; but late that night he came to his desk once more, to write the story of the accident to Corporal Gray; and the tale that he wrote had been already put into writing by Tom Vanrevel as it fell from Crailey's lips, after the doctor had, come, so that none might doubt it. No one did doubt it. What reason had Mr. Carewe to injure Crailey Gray? Only five in Rouen knew the truth; for Nelson had gone with his master, and, except Mamie, the other servants of the Carewe household had been among the crowd in front of the Rouen House when the shot was fired.

So the story went over the town: how Crailey had called to say good-by to Mrs. Tanberry; how Mr. Carewe happened to be examining the musket his father had carried in 1812, when the weapon was accidentally discharged, the ball entering Crailey's breast; how Mr. Carewe, stricken with remorse and horror over this frightful misfortune, and suffering too severe anguish of mind to remain upon the scene, of the tragedy which his carelessness had made, had fled, attended by his servant; and how they had leaped aboard the evening boat as it was pulling out, and were now on their way down the river.

And this was the story, too, that Tom told Fanchon; for it was he who brought her to Crailey. Through the long night she knelt at Crailey's side, his hand always pressed to her breast or cheek, her eyes always upward, and her lips moving with her prayers, not for Crailey to be spared, but that the Father would take good care of him in heaven till she came. "I had already given him up," she said to Tom, meekly, in a small voice. "I knew it was to come, and perhaps this way is better than that—I thought it would be far away from me. Now I can be with him, and perhaps I shall have him a little longer, for he was to have gone away before noon."

The morning sun rose upon a fair world, gay with bird-chatterings from the big trees of the Carewe place, and pleasant with the odors of Miss Betty's garden, and Crailey, lying upon the bed of the man who had shot him, hearkened and smiled good-by to the summer he loved; and, when the day broke, asked that the bed be moved so that he might lie close by the window. It was Tom who had borne him to that room. "I have carried him before this," he said, waving the others aside.

Not long after sunrise, when the bed had been moved near the window, Crailey begged Fanchon to bring him a miniature of his mother which he had given her, and urged her to go for it herself; he wanted no hands but hers to touch it, he said. And when she had gone he asked to be left alone with Tom.

"Give me your hand, Tom," he said, faintly. "I'd like to keep hold of it a minute or so. I couldn't have said that yesterday, could I, without causing us both horrible embarrassment? But I fancy I can now, because I'm done for. That's too bad, isn't it? I'm very young, after all. Do you remember what poor Andre Chenier said as he went up to be guillotined?—' There were things in this head of mine!' But I want to tell you what's been the matter with me. It was just my being a bad sort of poet. I suppose that I've never loved anyone; yet I've cared more deeply than other men for every lovely thing I ever saw, and there's so little that hasn't loveliness in it. I'd be ashamed not to have cared for the beauty in all the women I've made love to—but about this one—the most beautiful of all—I—"

"She will understand!" said Tom, quickly.

"She will—yes—she's wise and good. If Fanchon knew, there wouldn't be even a memory left to her—and I don't think she'd live. And do you know, I believe I've done a favor for Miss Betty in getting myself shot; Carewe will never come back. Tom, was ever a man's knavery so exactly the architect of his own destruction as mine? And for what gain? Just the excitement of the comedy from day to day!— for she was sure to despise me as soon as she knew—and the desire to hear her voice say another kindly thing to me—and the everlasting perhaps in every woman, and this one the Heart's Desire of all the world! Ah, well! Tell me—I want to hear it from you—how many hours does the doctor say?"

"Hours, Crailey?" Tom's hand twitched pitifully in the other's feeble grasp.

"I know it's only a few."

"They're all fools, doctors!" exclaimed Vanrevel, fiercely.

"No, no. And I know that nothing can be done. You all see it, and you want me to go easily—or you wouldn't let me have my own way so much! It frightens me, I own up, to think that so soon I'll be wiser than the wisest in the world. Yet I always wanted to know. I've sought and I've sought—but now to go out alone on the search—it must be the search, for the Holy Grail—I—"

"Please don't talk," begged Tom, in a broken whisper. "For mercy's sake, lad. It wears on you so."

Crailey laughed weakly. "Do you think I could die peacefully without talking a great deal? There's one thing I want, Tom. I want to see all of them once more, all the old friends that are going down the river at noon. What harm could it do? I want them to come by here on their way to the boat, with the band and the new flag. But I want the band to play cheerfully! Ask 'em to play 'Rosin the Bow,' will you? I've never believed in mournfulness, and I don't want to see any of it now. It's the rankest impiety of all! And besides, I want to see them as they'll be when they come marching home—they must look gay!"

"Ah, don't, lad, don't!" Tom flung one arm about the other's shoulder and Crailey was silent, but rested his hand gently on his friend's head. In that attitude Fanchon found them when she came.

The volunteers gathered at the court-house two hours before noon. They met each other dismally, speaking in undertones as they formed in lines of four, while their dispirited faces showed that the heart was out of them. Not so with the crowds of country folk and townspeople who lined the streets to see the last of them. For these, when the band came marching down the street and took its place, set up a royal cheering that grew louder as Jefferson Bareaud, the color-bearer, carried the flag to the head of the procession. With the recruits marched the veterans of 1812 and the Indian wars, the one-legged cobbler stumping along beside General

Trumble, who looked very dejected and old. The lines stood in silence, and responded to the cheering by quietly removing their hats; so that the people whispered that it was more like an Odd Fellows' Sunday funeral than the departure of enthusiastic patriots for the seat of war. General Trumble's was not the only sad face in the ranks; all were downcast and nervous, even those of the lads from the country, who had not known the comrade they were to leave behind.

Jefferson unfurled the flag; Marsh gave the word of command, the band began to play a quick-step, and the procession moved forward down the cheering lane of people, who waved little flags and handkerchiefs and threw their hats in the air as they shouted. But, contrary to expectation, the parade was not directly along Main Street to the river. "Right wheel! March!" commanded Tappingham, hoarsely, waving his sword, and Jefferson led the way into Carewe Street.

"For God's sake, don't cry now!" and Tappingham, with a large drop streaking down his own cheek, turned savagely upon Lieutenant Cummings. "That isn't what he wants. He wants to see us looking cheery and smiling. We can do it for him this once, I guess! I never saw him any other way."

"You look damn smiling yourself!" snuffled Will.

"I will when we turn in at the gates," retorted his Captain. "On my soul, I swear I'll kill every sniffling idiot that doesn't!—In line, there!" be stormed ferociously at a big recruit.

The lively strains of the band and the shouting of the people grew louder and louder in the room where Crailey lay. His eyes glistened as he heard, and he smiled, not the old smile of the worldly prelate, but merrily, like a child when music is heard. The room was darkened, save for the light of the one window which fell softly upon his head and breast and upon another fair head close to his, where Fanchon knelt. In the shadows at one end of the room were Miss Betty and Mrs. Tanberry and Mrs. Bareaud and the white-haired doctor who had said, "Let him have his own way in all he asks." Tom stood alone, close by the head of the couch.

"Hail to the band!" Crailey chuckled, softly. "How the rogues keep the time! It's 'Rosin the Bow,' all right! Ah, that is as it should be. Mrs. Tanberry, you and I have one thing in common, if you'll let me flatter myself so far: we've always believed in good cheer in spite of the devil and all, you and I, eh? The best of things, even if things are bad, dear lady, eh?"

"You darling vagabond!" Mrs. Tanberry murmured, trying to smile back to him.

"Hark to 'em!" said Crailey. "They're very near! Only hear the people cheer them! They'll 'march away so gaily,' won't they ?—and how right that is!" The vanguard appeared in the street, and over the hedge gleamed the oncoming banner, the fresh colors flying out on a strong breeze. Crailey greeted it with a breathless cry. "There's the flag—look, Fanchon, your flag!—.waving above the hedge; and it's Jeff who carries it. Doesn't it always make you want to dance! Bravo, bravo!"

The procession halted for a moment in the street and the music ceased. Then, with a jubilant flourish of brass and the roll of drums, the band struck up "The Star Spangled Banner," and Jefferson Bareaud proudly led the way through the gates and down the driveway, the bright silk streaming overhead. Behind him briskly marched the volunteers, with heads erect and cheerful faces, as they knew Corporal Gray wished to see them, their Captain flourishing his sword in the air.

"Here they come! Do you see, Fanchon?" cried Crailey,

excitedly. "They are all there, Jeff and Tappingham, and the two Madrillons and Will, the dear old fellow—he'll never write a decent paragraph as long as he lives, God bless him!—and young Frank—what deviltries I've led the boy into!—and there's the old General, forgetting all the tiffs we've had. God bless them all and grant them all a safe return! What on earth are they taking off their hats for?—Ah, good-by, boys, good-by!"

They saw the white face at the window, and the slender hand fluttering its farewell, and Tappingham halted his men.

"Three times three for Corporal Gray!" he shouted, managing, somehow, to keep the smile upon his lips. "Three times three, and may he rejoin his company before we enter the Mexican capital!"

He beat the time for the thunderous cheers that they gave; the procession described a circle on the lawn, and then, with the band playing and colors flying, passed out of the gates and took up the march to the wharf.

"the flag, the flag!" whispered Crailey, following it with his eyes. "It shows that you helped make it, Fanchon, it's so beautiful. Ah, Tom, they've said we abused it, sometimes—it was only that we loved it so well we didn't like to see anyone make it look silly or mean. But, after all, no man can do that—no, nor no group of men, nor party! His voice grew louder as the last strains of the music came more faintly from the street. "They'll take your banner across the Rio Grande, Fanchon, but that is not all—some day its stars must spread over the world! Don't you all see that they will?"

After a little while, he closed his eyes with a sigh; the doctor bent over him quickly, and Miss Betty started forward unconsciously and cried out.

But the bright eyes opened again and fixed themselves upon her with all their old, gay inscrutability.

"Not yet," said Crailey. "Miss Carewe, may I tell you that I am sorry I could not have known you sooner? Perhaps you might have liked me for Fanchon's sake—I know you care for her."

"I do—I do!" she faltered. "I love her, and—ah!—I do like you, Mr. Gray, for I know you, though I never—met you until—last night. God bless you—God bless you!"

She wavered a moment, like a lily in the wind, and put out a hand blindly. "Not you!" she said sharply, as Tom Vanrevel started toward her. Mrs. Tanberry came quickly and put an arm about her, and together they went out of the room.

"You must be good to her, Tom," said Crailey then, in a very low voice.

"I!" answered Tom, gently. "There was never a chance of that, lad."

"Listen," whispered Crailey. "Lean down—no—closer." He cast a quick glance at Fanchon, kneeling at the other side of the bed, her golden head on the white coverlet, her outstretched hand clutching his; and he spoke so close to Tom's ear and in so low a tone that only Tom could hear. "She never cared for me. She felt that she ought to—but that was only because I masqueraded in your history. She wanted to tell me before I went away that there was no chance for me. She was telling me that, when he called from the window. It was at the dance, the night before, that she knew. I think there has been someone else from the first—God send it's you! Did you speak to her that night or she to you?"

"Ah, no," said Tom Vanrevel. "All the others."

Mrs. Tanberry and Betty and Mr. Bareaud waited in the library, the two women huddled together on a sofa, with their arms round each other, and all the house was very still. By and by, they heard a prolonged, far-away cheering and the steamer's whistle, and knew that the boat was off. Half an hour later, Will Cummings came back alone, entered the room on tip-toe, and silently sank into a chair near Mr. Bareaud, with his face away from Miss Betty. He was to remain in Rouen another week, and join his regiment with Tom. None of the three appeared to notice his coming more than dimly, and he sat with his face bowed in his hands, and did not move.

Thus perhaps an hour passed, with only a sound of footsteps on the gravel of the driveway, now and then, and a low murmur of voices in the rear of the house where people came to ask after Crailey; and when the door of the room where he lay was opened, the four watchers started as at a loud explosion. It was Mrs. Bareaud and the old doctor, and they closed the door again, softly, and came in to the others. They had left Crailey alone with Fanchon and Tom Vanrevel, the two who loved him best.

The warm day beyond the windows became like Sunday, no voices sounded from without in the noon hush, though sometimes a little group of people would gather across the street to eye the house curiously and nod and whisper. The strong, blue shadows of the veranda pillars stole slowly across the white floor of the porch in a lessening slant, and finally lay all in a line, as the tall clock in a corner of the library asthmatically coughed the hour of noon. In this jarring discordance there was something frightful to Miss Betty. She rose abruptly, and, imperiously waving back Mrs. Tanberry, who would have detained her—for there was in her face and manner the incipient wildness of control over-strained to the breaking-point—she went hurriedly out of the room and out of the house, to the old bench in the garden. There she sank down, her face hidden in her arms; there on the spot where she had first seen Crailey Gray.

From there, too, had risen the serenade of the man she had spurned and insulted; and there she had come to worship the stars when Crailey bade her look to them. And now the strange young teacher was paying the bitter price for his fooleries—and who could doubt that the price was a bitter one? To have the spirit so suddenly, cruelly riven from the sprightly body that was, but a few hours ago, hale and alert, obedient to every, petty wish, could dance, run, and leap; to be forced with such hideous precipitation to leave the warm breath of June and undergo the lonely change, merging with the shadow; to be flung from the exquisite and commonplace day of sunshine into the appalling adventure that should not have been his for years—and hurled into it by what hand!—ah, bitter, bitter price for a harlequinade! And, alas, alas! for the brave harlequin!

A gentle touch fell upon her shoulder, and Miss Betty sprang to her feet and screamed. It was Nelson who stood before her, hat in hand, his head deeply bowed.

"Is he with you?" she cried, clutching at the bench for support.

"No'm," answered the old man, humbly. "I reckon we all ain' goin' see dat man no mo'."

"Where is he?"

"On de way, honey, on de way."

"The way—to Rouen!" she gasped.

"No'm; he goin' cross de big water." He stretched out his hand and pointed solemnly to the east. "Him an' me we cotch de boat, an' yo' pa mek 'em taken de hosses on bode. Den we git off at Leeville, five mile' down de rivuh, an' yo' pa hol' de boat whiles I rid back alone an' git de news, an' what de tale is you all is tole, f'um ole Mist' Chen'eth; an' Mist' Chen'eth, he rid back wid me an' see yo' pa at Leeville, an' dey talk in de shed by de landin', an' yo' pa tell Mist' Chen'eth what 'rangements he goin' make wid de proprety. 'Den he git on de boat ag'in an' dey sto't her agoin'; an' he ain' wave no good-by, ner say no mo' wu'ds. Mist' Chen'eth rid back whens de light come; but I res' de hosses an' come back slow, 'case I ponduh on de worl', an' I mighty sorry fer yo' pa, Missy. He am' comin' back no mo', honey, an' Miz Tanberry an' me an' Mamie, we goin' take keer er you. Yo' pa gone back dah to de F'enchmun, whuh he 'uz a young man. He mighty sick, an' he scairt, honey; an' he ain' goin' git ovah dat, neider. 'Peah to me, Missy, like he done had a vizhum er he own soul, when he come an' look down at dat young man layin' on de grass, las' night!"

The old fellow bent his back before her in a solemn bow, as a feudal retainer in allegiance to the heir, but more in deference to the sorrow written upon her, and respecting its magnitude. With no words of comfort, for he knew she wanted only to be alone, he moved away, with infirm steps and shaking head, toward the rear of the house.

Miss Betty threw herself upon the bench again, face downward in her arms. And still the house lay in silence under the sunshine.

An hour had passed, and the shadows slanted strongly to the east, when the stillness was broken by a sound, low and small at first, then rising fearfully, a long, quavering wail of supreme anguish, that clutched and shook the listener's heart. No one could have recognized the voice as Fanchon's, yet everyone who heard it knew that it was hers; and that the soul of Crailey Gray had gone out upon the quest for the Holy Grail.

Miss Betty's hands clenched convulsively round the arm of the bench and a fit of shuddering seized her as if with the grip of a violent chill, though her eyes were dry. Then she lay quiet.

A long time afterward, she became aware of a step that paced the garden path behind her, and turned her face upon her arm so that she saw, but made no other motion. It was Tom Vanrevel, walking slowly up and down, his hands behind his back and his hat pulled far down over his eyes. He had not seen her.

She rose and spoke his name.

He turned and came to her. "Almost at the very last," he said, "Crailey whispered to me that be knew you thought him a great scamp, but to tell you to be sure to remember that it was all true about the stars."

CHAPTER XX

"GOODBY"

It was between twilight and candlelight, the gentle half-hour when the kind old Sand Man steals up the stairs of houses where children are; when rustic lovers stroll with slow and quiet steps down country lanes, and old bachelors are loneliest and dream of the things that might have been. Through the silence of the clear dusk came the whistle of the evening boat that was to bear Tom Vanrevel through the first stage of his long journey to the front of war, and the sound fell cheerlessly upon Miss Betty's ear, as she stood leaning against the sun-dial among the lilac bushes. Her attitude was not one of reverie; yet she stood very still, so still that, in the wan shimmer of the faded afterglow, one might have passed close by her and not have seen her. The long, dark folds of her gown showed faintly against the gray stone, and her arms, bare from the elbow, lay across the face of the dial with unrelaxed fingers clenching the cornice; her head drooping, not languidly but with tension, her eyes half-closed, showing the lashes against a pale cheek; and thus, motionless, leaning on the stone in the dusk, she might have been Sorrow's self.

She did not move, there was not even a flicker of the eyelashes, when a step sounded on the gravel of the driveway, and Vanrevel came slowly from the house. He stopped at a little distance from her, hat in hand. He was very thin, worn and old-looking, and in the failing light might have been taken for a tall, gentle ghost; yet his shoulders were squared and he held himself as straight as he had the first time she had ever seen him.

"Mrs. Tanberry told me I should find you here," he said, hesitatingly. "I have come to say good-by."

She did not turn toward him, nor did more than her lips move as she answered, "Good-by," and her tone was neither kind nor cold, but held no meaning whatever, not even indifference.

There was an interval of silence; then, without surprise, he walked sadly to the gate, paused, wheeled about suddenly, and returned with a quick, firm step.

"I will not go until I know that I do not misunderstand you," he said, "not even if there is only the slightest chance that I do. I want to say something to you, if you will let me, though naturally I remember you once asked me never to speak to you again. It is only that I have thought you did that under a misconception, or else I should still obey you. If you—"

"What is it that you wish to say?" Her tone was unchanged.

"Only that I think the hardest time for you has passed, and that—"

"Do you?" she interrupted.

"Yes," he returned, "the saddest of your life. I think it has gone forever. And I think that what will come to you will be all you wish for. There will be a little time of waiting—"

"Waiting for what?"

He drew a step nearer, and his voice became very gentle. "Cummings and I reach our regiment tomorrow night; and there in the camp is a group of men on the way to the war, and they all go the more bravely because each one of them has you in his heart;—not one but will be a better soldier because of you. I want you to believe that if all of them don't come back, yet the one whose safety you think of and fear for will return. For, you see, Crailey told me what you said to him when—when he met you here the last time. I have no way to know which of them you meant; but—he will come back to you! I am sure of it, because I believe you are to be happy. Ah, you've had your allotment of pain! After all, there is so little to regret: the town seems empty without its young men, yet you may rejoice, remembering how bravely they went and how gaily! They will sing half the way to Vera Cruz! You think it strange I should say there is so little to regret, when I've just laid away my best friend. It was his own doctrine, and the selfish personal grief and soreness grows less when I think of the gallant end he made, for it was he who went away most bravely and jauntily of all. Crailey was no failure, unless I let what he taught me go to no effect. And be sure he would have told you what I tell you now, that all is well with all in the world."

"Please!" she cried, with a quick intake of breath through closed teeth.

"I will do anything in the world to please you," he answered, sorrowfully. "Do you mean that—"

She turned at last and faced him, but without lifting her eyes. "Why did you come to say good-by to me?"

"I don't understand."

"I think you do." Her voice was cold and steady, but it was suddenly given to him to perceive that she was trembling from head to heel.

An exclamation of remorse broke from him.

"Ah! You came here to be alone. I—"

"Stop," she said. "You said good-by to me once before. Did you come to see—what you saw then?"

He fell back in utter amazement, but she advanced upon him swiftly. "Was it that?" she cried.

The unfortunate young man could make no reply, and remained unable to defend himself from her inexplicable attack.

"You have not forgotten," she went on, impetuously. "It was in the crowd, just before they gave you the flag. You saw—I know you saw—and it killed me with the shame of it! Now you come to me to look at the same thing again—and the boat waiting for you! Is it in revenge for that night at the Bareauds'? Perhaps this sounds wild to you—I can't help that—but why should you try to make it harder for me?"

From the porch came a strong voice: "Vanrevel!"

"God knows I haven't meant to," said Tom, in bitter pain. "I don't understand. It's Cummings calling for me; I'll go at once. I'd hoped, stupidly enough, that you would tell me whom it was you meant when you spoke to Crailey, so that I could help to make it surer that he'd come back to you. But I've only annoyed you. And you were here—away from the house—avoiding me, and fearing that I—"

"Vanrevel!" shouted William. (Mrs. Tanberry had not told Lieutenant Cummings where to find Miss Betty.)

"Fearing? Yes?"

"Fearing that I might discover you." He let his eyes rest on her loveliness once more, and as he saw that she still trembled, he extended his hand toward her in a gesture of infinite gentleness, like a blessing, heaved one great sigh, and, with head erect and body straight, set his face manfully toward the house.

He had taken three strides when his heart stopped beating at an ineffable touch on his sleeve. For, with a sharp cry, she sprang to him; and then, once more, among the lilac bushes where he had caught the white kitten, his hand was seized and held between two small palms, and the eyes of Miss Betty Carewe looked into the very soul of him.

"No!" she cried. "No! Fearing with a sick heart that you might not come!"

Her pale face, misty with sweetness, wavered before him in the dusk, and he lifted his shaking hand to his forehead; her own went with it, and the touch of that steadied him.

"You mean," he whispered, brokenly, "you mean that you—"

"Yes, always," she answered, rushing through the words, half in tears. "There was a little time when I loved what your life had been more than you. Ah, it was you that I saw in him. Yet it was not what you had done after all, but just you! I knew there could not be anyone else—though I thought it could never be you—that night, just before they gave the flag."

"We've little time, Vanrevel!" called the voice from the porch.

Tom's eyes filled slowly. He raised them and looked at the newly come stars. "Crailey, Crailey!" he murmured.

Her gaze followed his. "Ah, it's he—and they—that make me know you will come back to me!" she said.

ABOUT THE AUTHOR

Newton Booth Tarkington (July 29, 1869 – May 19, 1946) was an American novelist and dramatist best known for his Pulitzer Prize-winning novels The Magnificent Ambersons and Alice Adams.

Booth Tarkington was born in Indianapolis, the son of John S. Tarkington and Elizabeth Booth Tarkington. He was named after his maternal uncle Newton Booth, then the governor of California. He first attended Purdue University but graduated from Princeton University in 1893. While at Princeton he was editor of the "Nassau Literary Magazine" and formed the Triangle Club. He was also voted the most popular man in his class. When Tarkington's class graduated in 1893 he lacked sufficient credits for a degree at Princeton, where he attended classes for two years. His later achievements, however, won him an honorary A.M. in 1899 and an honorary Litt.D. in 1918.

He was one of the most popular American novelists of his time, with The Two Vanrevels and Mary's Neck appearing on the annual best-seller lists nine times.

Tarkington donated substantially to Purdue University and has been recognized for his philanthropy. Tarkington Hall, an all-men's residence hall at Purdue, is named in honor of him.

Choose from Thousands of 1stWorldLibrary Classics By

A. M. Barnard
Ada Leverson
Adolphus William Ward
Aesop
Agatha Christie
Alexander Aaronsohn
Alexander Kielland
Alexandre Dumas
Alfred Gatty
Alfred Ollivant
Alice Duer Miller
Alice Turner Curtis
Alice Dunbar
Allen Chapman
Alleyne Ireland
Ambrose Bierce
Amelia E. Barr
Amory H. Bradford
Andrew Lang
Andrew McFarland Davis
Andy Adams
Angela Brazil
Anna Alice Chapin
Anna Sewell
Annie Besant
Annie Hamilton Donnell
Annie Payson Call
Annie Roe Carr
Annonaymous
Anton Chekhov
Archibald Lee Fletcher
Arnold Bennett
Arthur C. Benson
Arthur Conan Doyle
Arthur M. Winfield
Arthur Ransome
Arthur Schnitzler
Arthur Train
Atticus
B.H. Baden-Powell
B. M. Bower
B. C. Chatterjee
Baroness Emmuska Orczy
Baroness Orczy
Basil King
Bayard Taylor
Ben Macomber
Bertha Muzzy Bower
Bjornstjerne Bjornson

Booth Tarkington
Boyd Cable
Bram Stoker
C. Collodi
C. E. Orr
C. M. Ingleby
Carolyn Wells
Catherine Parr Traill
Charles A. Eastman
Charles Amory Beach
Charles Dickens
Charles Dudley Warner
Charles Farrar Browne
Charles Ives
Charles Kingsley
Charles Klein
Charles Hanson Towne
Charles Lathrop Pack
Charles Romyn Dake
Charles Whibley
Charles Willing Beale
Charlotte M. Braeme
Charlotte M. Yonge
Charlotte Perkins Stetson
Clair W. Hayes
Clarence Day Jr.
Clarence E. Mulford
Clemence Housman
Confucius
Coningsby Dawson
Cornelis DeWitt Wilcox
Cyril Burleigh
D. H. Lawrence
Daniel Defoe
David Garnett
Dinah Craik
Don Carlos Janes
Donald Keyhoe
Dorothy Kilner
Dougan Clark
Douglas Fairbanks
E. Nesbit
E. P. Roe
E. Phillips Oppenheim
E. S. Brooks
Earl Barnes
Edgar Rice Burroughs
Edith Van Dyne
Edith Wharton

Edward Everett Hale
Edward J. O'Biren
Edward S. Ellis
Edwin L. Arnold
Eleanor Atkins
Eleanor Hallowell Abbott
Eliot Gregory
Elizabeth Gaskell
Elizabeth McCracken
Elizabeth Von Arnim
Ellem Key
Emerson Hough
Emilie F. Carlen
Emily Bronte
Emily Dickinson
Enid Bagnold
Enilor Macartney Lane
Erasmus W. Jones
Ernie Howard Pie
Ethel May Dell
Ethel Turner
Ethel Watts Mumford
Eugene Sue
Eugenie Foa
Eugene Wood
Eustace Hale Ball
Evelyn Everett-green
Everard Cotes
F. H. Cheley
F. J. Cross
F. Marion Crawford
Fannie E. Newberry
Federick Austin Ogg
Ferdinand Ossendowski
Fergus Hume
Florence A. Kilpatrick
Fremont B. Deering
Francis Bacon
Francis Darwin
Frances Hodgson Burnett
Frances Parkinson Keyes
Frank Gee Patchin
Frank Harris
Frank Jewett Mather
Frank L. Packard
Frank V. Webster
Frederic Stewart Isham
Frederick Trevor Hill
Frederick Winslow Taylor

Friedrich Kerst
Friedrich Nietzsche
Fyodor Dostoyevsky
G.A. Henty
G.K. Chesterton
Gabrielle E. Jackson
Garrett P. Serviss
Gaston Leroux
George A. Warren
George Ade
Geroge Bernard Shaw
George Cary Eggleston
George Durston
George Ebers
George Eliot
George Gissing
George MacDonald
George Meredith
George Orwell
George Sylvester Viereck
George Tucker
George W. Cable
George Wharton James
Gertrude Atherton
Gordon Casserly
Grace E. King
Grace Gallatin
Grace Greenwood
Grant Allen
Guillermo A. Sherwell
Gulielma Zollinger
Gustav Flaubert
H. A. Cody
H. B. Irving
H.C. Bailey
H. G. Wells
H. H. Munro
H. Irving Hancock
H. R. Naylor
H. Rider Haggard
H. W. C. Davis
Haldeman Julius
Hall Caine
Hamilton Wright Mabie
Hans Christian Andersen
Harold Avery
Harold McGrath
Harriet Beecher Stowe
Harry Castlemon
Harry Coghill
Harry Houidini

Hayden Carruth
Helent Hunt Jackson
Helen Nicolay
Hendrik Conscience
Hendy David Thoreau
Henri Barbusse
Henrik Ibsen
Henry Adams
Henry Ford
Henry Frost
Henry James
Henry Jones Ford
Henry Seton Merriman
Henry W Longfellow
Herbert A. Giles
Herbert Carter
Herbert N. Casson
Herman Hesse
Hildegard G. Frey
Homer
Honore De Balzac
Horace B. Day
Horace Walpole
Horatio Alger Jr.
Howard Pyle
Howard R. Garis
Hugh Lofting
Hugh Walpole
Humphry Ward
Ian Maclaren
Inez Haynes Gillmore
Irving Bacheller
Isabel Cecilia Williams
Isabel Hornibrook
Israel Abrahams
Ivan Turgenev
J.G.Austin
J. Henri Fabre
J. M. Barrie
J. M. Walsh
J. Macdonald Oxley
J. R. Miller
J. S. Fletcher
J. S. Knowles
J. Storer Clouston
J. W. Duffield
Jack London
Jacob Abbott
James Allen
James Andrews
James Baldwin

James Branch Cabell
James DeMille
James Joyce
James Lane Allen
James Lane Allen
James Oliver Curwood
James Oppenheim
James Otis
James R. Driscoll
Jane Abbott
Jane Austen
Jane L. Stewart
Janet Aldridge
Jens Peter Jacobsen
Jerome K. Jerome
Jessie Graham Flower
John Buchan
John Burroughs
John Cournos
John F. Kennedy
John Gay
John Glasworthy
John Habberton
John Joy Bell
John Kendrick Bangs
John Milton
John Philip Sousa
John Taintor Foote
Jonas Lauritz Idemil Lie
Jonathan Swift
Joseph A. Altsheler
Joseph Carey
Joseph Conrad
Joseph E. Badger Jr
Joseph Hergesheimer
Joseph Jacobs
Jules Vernes
Julian Hawthrone
Julie A Lippmann
Justin Huntly McCarthy
Kakuzo Okakura
Karle Wilson Baker
Kate Chopin
Kenneth Grahame
Kenneth McGaffey
Kate Langley Bosher
Kate Langley Bosher
Katherine Cecil Thurston
Katherine Stokes
L. A. Abbot
L. T. Meade

L. Frank Baum
Latta Griswold
Laura Dent Crane
Laura Lee Hope
Laurence Housman
Lawrence Beasley
Leo Tolstoy
Leonid Andreyev
Lewis Carroll
Lewis Sperry Chafer
Lilian Bell
Lloyd Osbourne
Louis Hughes
Louis Joseph Vance
Louis Tracy
Louisa May Alcott
Lucy Fitch Perkins
Lucy Maud Montgomery
Luther Benson
Lydia Miller Middleton
Lyndon Orr
M. Corvus
M. H. Adams
Margaret E. Sangster
Margret Howth
Margaret Vandercook
Margaret W. Hungerford
Margret Penrose
Maria Edgeworth
Maria Thompson Daviess
Mariano Azuela
Marion Polk Angellotti
Mark Overton
Mark Twain
Mary Austin
Mary Catherine Crowley
Mary Cole
Mary Hastings Bradley
Mary Roberts Rinehart
Mary Rowlandson
M. Wollstonecraft Shelley
Maud Lindsay
Max Beerbohm
Myra Kelly
Nathaniel Hawthrone
Nicolo Machiavelli
O. F. Walton
Oscar Wilde

Owen Johnson
P.G. Wodehouse
Paul and Mabel Thorne
Paul G. Tomlinson
Paul Severing
Percy Brebner
Percy Keese Fitzhugh
Peter B. Kyne
Plato
Quincy Allen
R. Derby Holmes
R. L. Stevenson
R. S. Ball
Rabindranath Tagore
Rahul Alvares
Ralph Bonehill
Ralph Henry Barbour
Ralph Victor
Ralph Waldo Emmerson
Rene Descartes
Ray Cummings
Rex Beach
Rex E. Beach
Richard Harding Davis
Richard Jefferies
Richard Le Gallienne
Robert Barr
Robert Frost
Robert Gordon Anderson
Robert L. Drake
Robert Lansing
Robert Lynd
Robert Michael Ballantyne
Robert W. Chambers
Rosa Nouchette Carey
Rudyard Kipling
Saint Augustine
Samuel B. Allison
Samuel Hopkins Adams
Sarah Bernhardt
Sarah C. Hallowell
Selma Lagerlof
Sherwood Anderson
Sigmund Freud
Standish O'Grady
Stanley Weyman
Stella Benson
Stella M. Francis

Stephen Crane
Stewart Edward White
Stijn Streuvels
Swami Abhedananda
Swami Parmananda
T. S. Ackland
T. S. Arthur
The Princess Der Ling
Thomas A. Janvier
Thomas A Kempis
Thomas Anderton
Thomas Bailey Aldrich
Thomas Bulfinch
Thomas De Quincey
Thomas Dixon
Thomas H. Huxley
Thomas Hardy
Thomas More
Thornton W. Burgess
U. S. Grant
Upton Sinclair
Valentine Williams
Various Authors
Vaughan Kester
Victor Appleton
Victor G. Durham
Victoria Cross
Virginia Woolf
Wadsworth Camp
Walter Camp
Walter Scott
Washington Irving
Wilbur Lawton
Wilkie Collins
Willa Cather
Willard F. Baker
William Dean Howells
William le Queux
W. Makepeace Thackeray
William W. Walter
William Shakespeare
Winston Churchill
Yei Theodora Ozaki
Yogi Ramacharaka
Young E. Allison
Zane Grey